ROMANCE AND REVOLUTION

A Leap of Faith at the Iranian National Ballet

Published by Mantua Books

Brantford Ontario N3T 6J9

www.mantuabooks.com

Library and Archives Canada Cataloguing in Publication

Symonds, Clair, 1953-
    Romance and revolution : a leap of faith at the Iranian National Ballet / Clair Symonds.

ISBN 978-0-9869414-2-9

    1. Symonds, Clair, 1953-. 2. Symonds, Clair, 1953- -- Marriage. 3. Iran--History--Revolution, 1979. 4. Ballerinas--Iran--Biography. 5. Jews--Iran--Biography. 6. Iranian National Ballet. I. Title.

DS318.84.S95A3 2012   955.05'4092   C2012-902252-7

CLAIR SYMONDS

She might as well have been born with *pointe* shoes on her feet. For Clair Symonds was destined, it seems, to spend the best part of her life in dance studios and ballet companies. Having grown up in apartheid South Africa - she enrolled at the Royal Ballet School in London at the age of 17.

Two years later she successfully auditioned for the Iranian National Ballet Company - even though she had little idea of where that country was located. Performing soloist roles in many of the major classics, including *Giselle*, *Swan Lake* and *Les Sylphides*, she met and married her husband Arash Alizadeh whilst working there.

She was subsequently engaged as a lead in the Irish Ballet Company based in Cork. She travelled all over the world with the Alexander Roy London Ballet Theatre performing in India, Taiwan, Malta and Brunei. She has appeared regularly at the London Coliseum as a dancer with the English National Opera -performing in numerous operas including *The Mikado* on no less than 85 occasions.

Although she has always claimed that her 'brains were in her feet', she recently disproved that assertion by completing a Bachelor of Arts degree with the Open University.

Contents

PREFACE

It might sound something of a contradiction. But despite growing up with a dance and stage background, I have never really been one to push myself forward or seek the limelight in any way. That remains the case to this day. But over the years, as I related my story from time to time, people would often encourage me to put pen to paper with a view to allowing others to see what it was I had to say. It took me the best part of two decades to find the courage to heed their advice. Whether or not these people were right to spur me on is of course for others to decide. What I am trying to say, I guess, is that I hope I have done a good job and that you will enjoy the read.

Whatever the case it's been wonderful revisiting my South African and Iranian days although, like many things in life, delving into the past brings with it both risks and rewards, as memories are aroused from their slumber and dormant feelings likewise are brought back to the fore.

Of course my life does not grind to a halt in 1982 - after all, that was some thirty years ago - so it goes without saying that much has happened since. But the book does indeed stop at that date on the grounds that that is where my Iranian adventure more or less comes to a close. I am really hoping, however, that readers will see that the issues addressed in the book - notably relationships between Muslims and Jews - are very much alive and kicking and relevant to the world of today. More so now, in fact, than ever. But because of the distinctly unpleasant nature of the current regime in Iran I have altered the names of some people mentioned in the text with a view to protecting their true identities.

There are many people I would like to thank for their help and encouragement in seeing to it that this book eventually came to see the light of day. It was a bit of a battle, I have to say. The key players will know who they are and would, I think, shy away from being mentioned or thanked in any way. Still, there are so many individuals who helped me that rather than list the precise nature of their assistance I am simply going to record my gratitude to them all. And alphabetically to boot. So its an enormous thank you to Mike

Adamson, Jeremy Allen, Soheila Ardalan, Tim Barlass, Ted Belman, Jack Bordan, Professor Goel Cohen, Joelle Cohen, Natalie Conway, Ora Cummings, Peter Eftemeijer, Chaya Grodner, Professor Israel Finkelstein, Sheila Frank, Martine and Peter Halban, Gerald Jacobs, Gabrielle Johnson, Sylvia Josephs, Jackie Jurke, Jeffrey Kaiser, Fran Kaufmann, Jeff Lewis, Andrew Lownie, Jonathan Margolis, Janet Matricciani, Naji Mrad, Ruth Pevsner, Zippy Porath, Professor Karen Ritchie, Andrew Roberts, Jeremy Robson, Robert Rosenstone, Howard Rotberg, Flore Scalbert, Robert Smith, Lord Steel, Anna Swan, Michael Symonds, Joshua Tallent, Andria Valentini, Professor Jonathan Waxman and Martin Weitz.   I am enormously grateful to you all.

C.S. Montpellier, France, Spring 2012

TO MY FATHER

PROLOGUE

The formal word for it is lapidation.   But most people know it as death by stoning.   Until recently the extent of my knowledge on this extremely gruesome subject happened to be drawn from the world of comedy - a scene from the satirical film *Monty Python's Life of Brian*, to be precise, when John Cleese, kitted out as a Roman official, hilariously tries to organize the stoning of a character known as Matthias by a group of women disguised as men.   In keeping with the best traditions of Python humour, the script writers came up with a less than convincing legal defence for the prospective victim, who looked on bemused whilst shackled in chains throughout.   'Look', Matthias pleads, 'All that happened was that I'd had a lovely supper and said to my wife 'that piece of halibut was good enough for Jehovah'.

I was at my home in Montpellier, France, listening online to the Today Programme on BBC Radio 4 when I heard the name Sakineh Mohammadi Ashtiani mentioned for the first time.   It was during the summer of 2011.   I could not believe my ears - that a 43 year old Iranian mother of two convicted of adultery had been sentenced to death by stoning.   Suddenly the subject didn't seem quite such a laughing matter.   The same court in the north-western city of Tabriz had already seen to it that she receive 99 lashes, a punishment which her then teenage son Sajjad Mohammedie went out of his way to observe, reluctantly concluding that he could not leave his mother alone in the face of such suffering.   There was an international outcry on Sakineh's behalf.   Not just in relation to the barbarity of the sentence imposed but because her confession was in fact no confession at all, having been extracted under duress and torture.

Of course you don't need to spend vast amounts of time on Google to know that stoning is one of the cruellest forms of punishment to have been dreamed up in the whole of human history.   But the more I read about it, the more I saw how brutal and sadistic it was, not least because the overwhelming majority of victims of stoning are women. During *Rajm* - Arabic for stoning - the condemned person is made to wear a white sheet before being buried in a hole in the ground.   Males up to the waist, females to the chest.   Rules and regulations also exist

1

as to who can throw what and when: the stones should not be so big that they kill the victim quickly. But nor should they be too small either, pebbles are not allowed. The process of being tortured to death can then get underway. The object of the exercise could hardly be more clear - to kill the person gradually and with the utmost pain. Death can take up to an hour.

I joined a lobby group, the International Committee Against Stoning, which happens to be based in Germany, and I could hardly put my name down quickly enough as a signatory for the Save Sakineh Mohammadi Ashtiani Campaign. Recently I learned that her sentence had been commuted to death by hanging -the most bizarre 'good news' story I think I have ever heard. In a rather unsubtle attempt to counter the growing numbers of those campaigning for her release, she was even taken from her prison cell so that she could participate in a state-sponsored television reconstruction of the alleged murder of her husband, the programme being broadcast, somewhat bizarrely, on world Human Rights Day. In any event, her case is ongoing and many high profile people have, thankfully, given their backing to these campaigns. More recently the Iranian authorities have apparently stayed her execution indefinitely, in response to a highly effective international campaign. But she continues to languish in jail.

For one's heart not to go out to the plight of Sakineh surely shows a lack of humanity and compassion. But her suffering unsettled me far more than I could have imagined. Was this because I had once been a visitor to Tabriz, Iran's fourth largest city? I can still single out Tabrizi rugs to this day, identifiable by their ivory backgrounds with blue, rose and indigo motifs. Thinking of Tabriz led me inexorably to Tehran - the Iranian capital which had once been my home. And Tehran in turn took me to Talar Roudaki, formerly Iran's premier centre for the performing arts and where, for some years, I was employed by the Iranian National Ballet. My background and training is rooted firmly in classical dance. So *dancey*, in fact, that it is now a matter of some regret that I paid little attention to academic study. But for some reason I have always retained the words of the German Jewish essayist Kurt Tocholsky, that *a country is not only what it does but also what it tolerates.* On that litmus test of

2

liberality the current regime in Iran should surely hang its head in shame. With all forms of public dance banned in the aftermath of the Iranian Revolution, Talar Roudaki now serves as a centre for Islamic gatherings. I am sure that Sakineh might also have something to say, given the opportunity, about the regime's lack of respect for the most basic human right of all - the right to life. Whatever the case, reading about Sakineh and campaigning on her behalf was taking me swiftly back to Iran, a country whose culture, language and people I had come to love. Although imprisoned and languishing on death row, it was as if she were accompanying me on a return trip to Talar Roudaki, a bizarre fusion of present and past. I remember getting on that jumbo jet and flying out to Tehran as if it were yesterday. Even though it was four decades ago.

Chapter 1: Terminal Three, Heathrow Airport, London: July 1972
40 years earlier

It was all my fault. All of my own doing. But now the enormity of the situation which I had gone out of my way to create suddenly began to hit home. Worse still, there appeared to be no escape. I came to the conclusion that I had only one option - to act as any self-respecting teenager would in front of their parents and do my level best to conceal the fact that I was surely on the verge of making a monumental mistake.

In less than an hour I would be heading out towards Iran and the Middle East, a country I'd barely heard of and a region I knew almost nothing about. Was it wise for a Jewish girl to be setting off to a Muslim country? Family and friends had repeatedly suggested that it was not. But in keeping with the greater part of unsolicited advice received at that time, I ignored them. Because the truth was that from the moment the director of the Iranian National Ballet had offered me a position in his company my mind was made up.
Photos of Persian dancers performing lavish productions of classics such as *Swan Lake* and *Giselle* had been spread out rather ostentatiously on a coffee table in the compact room allocated to Miss Fewster, the principal of the Royal Ballet School. Not that the photographs were necessary, I was already tingling with excitement at the prospect of finally becoming a professional ballet dancer - the fulfilment of my childhood dream.

But now, at Heathrow airport, I was anxious and on edge. I glanced nervously at the seasoned travellers heading out on the flight to Iran. I sensed that even for those who had made countless round trips to Tehran there was an atmosphere of excitement and anticipation as we made our way through the drab facilities of Iran Air on that early July morning back in 1972.

As I caught the eye of other young dancers who, like me, were bound for the ballet company in Tehran, I tried not to nestle too closely to my parents, who evidently had their own strategy for putting on a brave face. I did my best to keep a respectable teenage distance, but could feel the seeds of panic quietly taking hold. There could be no going back now. That was it. The decision taken, the die cast. Still, I was struggling to relinquish feelings of uncertainty in my apparent headlong rush to become a young adult anxious to establish her rightful place in the grown-up world.

I dreaded saying goodbye to my parents; the sadness they struggled to conceal was palpable. Having spent almost the entirety of his post-war years in South Africa, my father maintained a stiff upper lip colonial mentality and English reserve. He had lost most of his dark hair as a young man but his strong and sturdy frame belied the physique of a man now in his late fifties. Finally it was time to board the plane. As if in a last bid to stop me from departing, he put his arms around me. 'Take care of yourself,' he said, with uncharacteristic emotion behind his words. 'I believe there is an ancient Jewish community in Tehran - why don't you visit the main synagogue there and touch base with them?' I nodded in approval at my father's suggestion. 'But whatever you do, never forget if you need us we are only a phone call away.'

As I kissed my mother goodbye I felt a slight tightening in my throat. In a barely audible croak and fighting back tears, I said, 'Of course I will write. And phone. I promise.' I had little idea at that time that thousands of letters would make their way back and forth between London and Tehran. When I turned around for one final wave, I hoped they couldn't see my tears or the artificial smile set on my face.

The Rolls Royce engines of the Boeing 747 powered the aircraft along the runway. As it climbed into the sky I noticed that the plane was full to capacity with Iranians and Europeans heading towards a country synonymous with Persian carpets, exotic spices, hubbly bubbly and the Peacock Throne, the name of an Indian Mogul sovereign but popularly used to describe the rule of a powerful emperor known as the Shah of Iran. Such was the sum total of my knowledge in respect of one of the world's most ancient civilisations.

Finally relaxing into my thoughts, I sensed the nutty aroma of freshly-served coffee. It was soon accompanied by another equally comforting stimulant - the clattering and clinking of cutlery, crockery and glassware precariously perched on the air hostesses' trolleys and being pushed along the aircraft's narrow aisles. It was a sound that brought rapid relief and reassurance. At least to me. Yet such a sound belonged not to Persia and the east but to Africa and the south - to my native South Africa, to be precise.

Chapter 2:   Richard and Katie

For here at 35,000 feet above ground-level and travelling at a speed of almost 500 miles per hour I was being served.   The theme of service had been one of the constants of my childhood in Johannesburg.   Why dwell on the uncertainties of the future when such speedy security could be provided from the past?   I turned my thoughts away from the air hostesses and towards Richard, the black servant of my childhood, a man I had come to love.

Of course Richard was no air steward - as if South African Airways would ever have employed blacks on the front line of the aviation industry - but his routine of domestic service was by no means dissimilar. Every day, with almost military precision, he would carefully wheel out a generously prepared trolley from the kitchen towards the veranda where he had meticulously laid out four places for my family's one o'clock lunch. It never crossed my mind that being served in this manner was anything other than the norm. I was a child of apartheid and it didn't dawn on me that the nationalist government's policy of white domination and institutionalised racism was wrong - even to the slightest degree.   Of course I'd heard of Nelson Mandela and took comfort from the knowledge that the country's most notorious terrorist was locked up on Robben Island in one of the world's most secure prisons a few miles off the coast of Cape Town.

It's not difficult to recall how Richard came into the lives of my parents, Sheila and 'Duke' Symonds, and mine. His brother had responded swiftly to news speeding along the black grapevine that a family in Johannesburg was looking to employ a male servant as soon as possible. It wasn't long before my father answered the door to an African man in his late twenties. He was of tall stature and muscular build, his pierced ears bearing large plug earrings, the hallmark of Zulu tradition.   His deep-set eyes conveyed the traumas and uncertainties of life on the wrong side of apartheid.   Both my older brother Michael and I were keen to take hidden glimpses from a cautious distance towards this most unusual petitioner at our front door.

'Excuse me *baas*,' he said rather awkwardly, quickly removing his cap and lowering his eyes.

'Yes, good morning' returned my father. I had always adored his plumb English accent. Despite a life-time of servility, it was not difficult to detect that the uninvited caller brought with him an innate sense of pride, as he continued in steady but broken English.

'My name Joshua Ngshlonga. I work just over the road on Louis Botha Avenue. I hear you look for some help, *baas*, in the house and with garden.

'That's right', replied my father courteously.

'My youngest brother Richard very hard worker with cattle and goat in village. He very happy to help and he learn quickly how to work in house'. It began to emerge that Richard was no more than sixteen or seventeen - whatever the case it was clear that he was seeking his first paid employment with a 'white-European' family.

'Well Joshua, why don't you bring Richard along? We'll give him a trial run'.

I looked at Michael in surprise at my father's unusually hasty decision.

'If he's up to the job - as you seem to think - then we'll keep him. He'll have his own room at the back of the house and of course his meals provided.'

'Thank you *baas*'.

My father continued. 'His salary will be sixty rand a month, and we'll see how things go.'

'Yes *baas* - thank you *baas*.'

'And just before you go, Joshua, does your brother speak any English?'

'Oh no, *baas*, but I know he clever, he learn to speak English quickly.'

And with that he left, placing his cap comfortably back on his head.

A few weeks later a bemused and very young looking Zulu boy arrived at our home in the middle-class white suburb of Houghton. Richard was the youngest of five brothers. Most of his siblings had left the *kraal* to find work, some in the nearby city of Durban, others further afield in the Transvaal. His remote shanty village was situated in the undulating mountainous region of Zululand. With no more than the clothes he stood up in and what remained of the money my parents had sent him for the journey, he'd made his way north to our house in the affluent commercial heartland of South Africa and the mining business city of Johannesburg. Located in the mineral-loaded Witwatersrand range of hills, Johannesburg had become rich off the back of its gold and diamond trades. Needless to say, none of this wealth had trickled down to Zululand and thus Richard's way.

Richard had seen neither electricity nor running water and his big inquisitive eyes would open even wider when, as if by magic, he realised he could make light appear at the flick of a switch. 'Ho', he would exclaim with delight, each flick of the switch accompanied by an enormous smile. Not that our cook Katie was impressed by his antics. 'Ho' won't get the work done,' she snapped at him in their melodic mother tongue of isiZulu, '… so go and pick some *mealies* from the garden for the boss's lunch.'

Skinny, almost toothless and not averse to a tipple, this ageless African lady considered herself the undisputed Head of Kitchen and greatly resented interference from any outside party, especially my mother. 'Miss Sheila,' she would announce imperiously, 'you stay out of my kitchen and I'll stay out of your dance studio.' It was a deal my mother was more than willing to sign up to - less time in the kitchen meant more teaching time and which was most certainly fine by her.

Richard served us from the trolley and then quickly retreated to the kitchen and Katie. At the end of lunch my mother would ring a silver bell, a signal for the table to be cleared. The laws of apartheid ran right through our front lounge and beyond, ensuring that whilst Richard and Katie were entitled to walk through our living room at the sound of a bell to clear up our lunch dishes and complete every other conceivable domestic chore, they were not allowed to sleep under the same roof as us. It was one particularly unpleasant provision of the 1953 Reservation of Separate Amenities Act at work. Not that I knew, as a 6-year-old girl, about the intricacies of apartheid legislation. What I did know was that their living quarters were tucked away at the back of our house. In stark contrast to our sizeable residence with its tennis court and extensive gardens, their small and dingy single bedrooms came with nothing more than an outside toilet and shower, both of which were basic, cold and colourless. I didn't question this enforced segregation or try to familiarise myself with the complex workings of South African politics. I simply accepted that Katie and Richard were an integral part of our family, there to help around the house but also available for company and companionship. Richard, Katie and I had at least one thing in common: we were all singularly ignorant of the detailed provisions of the vast range of laws ensuring not only that South Africa's racial groups were kept apart but the carefully crafted legislation also seeing to it that the black population would forever remain at the very base of the miserable racial pyramid known as apartheid.

I would often while away the hours sitting on Katie's ruffled bed where she kindly allowed me to dig into her lunch bowl of *mealie-pap* with my bare hands, soaking up the scrumptious stewed meat covered in a tasty sauce. I always looked forward to the times when her daughter, Louisa, would pay us a surprise visit. Her radiant face was a perfect oval with long eye lashes shading her large dark brown eyes, her silky skin as soft as satin. She was in her early teens and as kind as she was beautiful. When my father was in his garage at the back of our house, servicing the engine of a customer's Rover - his particular speciality - or my mother busily absorbed in her dance studio from dawn to dusk, it was Louisa who patiently helped me with my times tables or accompanied me to piano lessons not far from our house. Together we would sing African songs she had taught me, *Tula Tu Tula baba* was my favourite, play ball games or jacks - anything to distract me from homework would do - as we whiled away the hours laughing in each other's company. So it came as something of a blow when Katie summarily banned her daughter from our house. Her crime? To have fallen pregnant. And with Richard as the prospective father to boot. I would never see her again and felt a great emptiness at the loss of my friend.

With the disappearance of my soul mate, I found myself spending next to no time on my homework and increasingly involved in watching my mother train students of all ages. I can't say precisely how it happened, I can't point to one moment in particular, but it had gradually begun to dawn on me what I wanted to do with my life. I wanted to dance.

Chapter 3: Don't put your Daughter on the Stage

My uncle used to delight in calling me string-bean on account of my slight build. Or *skinny-ma-links*. Of average height for six years of age, my short black curly hair steadfastly refused to grow long and straight despite my best efforts at willing it to do so each day. But only so that I could tie it in a bun and look like a proper ballet dancer. From the autumn of 1959 my mind was made up - my only ambition was to become a ballerina. An attainable objective, surely, in that my mother ran a highly sought-after dance school from our home, the Sheila Wartski Academy of Dance - she kept her maiden name for professional purposes. It should have been obvious that my mother was destined for a long and distinguished career in the world of dance on the grounds that she had managed, as a 10 year old performer, to catch the eye of Prince George, the Duke of Kent, when he visited her native Durban in 1934 and attended a show. With an innate sense of musical comedy, she had gone on to entertain Allied troops during the war and delighted audiences in Durban with a varied repertoire of antics relating to speech and dance.

But now, under her expert and watchful eye, the spacious living room of our Johannesburg home at 42, St John's Road had metamorphosed into a dance studio. The beautiful mahogany flooring was ripped up - with no thought for the skilled craftsmen who had laid it almost a quarter of a century earlier - to make way for a softer wood with more spring. The transformation was completed with the installation of enormous wall mirrors, ballet *barres* and a 1940s upright walnut Courtney, at which Mrs. Malamade, the school's elderly but eminently reliable pianist, played for classes.

Only a minority of the school's students found security and strength at the varnished maple ballet *barres*. This was entirely down to my mother's dominant personality which instilled in her students unconditional fear and respect but also great loyalty and affection for those strong or stubborn enough to survive being put through their paces. A demanding ballet mistress, she was a perfectionist with a singularity of purpose: to develop discipline and diligence and instil a love of dance even in her most reluctant recruits. And yet there were times when I would stare incredulously as she reduced less committed pupils to tears. It baffled me that they had such difficulty in reading my mother's mind. I could always tell when she was reaching the end of her tether, her voice would bounce off the studio walls before a familiar variety of one of the following assertions would reach the ears of her latest victim: 'there is no policeman at my door, you know' or 'if you don't like it … go home.' Many did.

Scores of indignant mothers stormed out of our house with their tearful, traumatised would-be ballerinas in tow. They let it be known, in no uncertain terms, that their gifted offspring would be seeking tuition elsewhere. But despite the dramas and rows occasionally played out in front of me, the studio held a magical magnetism. I absorbed the movements and music that permeated our household. They would soon come to represent my entire world outside of school.

My mother remained adamant. Although she had made an extraordinary success of her own career in dance and theatre, she had observed the disappointment of too many aspiring ballet dancers. No, ballet would not be her daughter's destiny. Instead I was to fulfil her long-since thwarted aspirations by becoming an actress. In a display of her affinity to the profession, I was named after Claire Bloom, the English actress chosen by Charlie Chaplin to appear in his film *Limelight*, an inspired casting that catapulted her to fame. The hope was that I would do likewise and enjoy similar onscreen success. Spelling, however, was not my mother's forte and she made one tiny mistake with a letter when registering my birth, omitting to add the final 'e'.

Not that I had any notion of what the world of theatre might have entailed, mesmerised as I was by the sight of feet pointing in ballet shoes, arms flowing elegantly through the air and heads spinning sharply to staccato music. In the event I had to wait until the grand old age of six-and-a-half before plucking up the courage to upset the status quo. Thoroughly fed up with my role as passive observer, I decided I was more than ready to join the dancers' ranks. Wearing my brother's over-sized hand-me-down tracksuit, bare foot and unobtrusive, I manoeuvred myself away from Mrs. Malamade's piano and into a class of eight-year-olds. Discreetly hidden at the back, I was happy to be ignored by teacher and pupils alike.

As the weeks and months progressed, it became increasingly difficult for my mother to overlook the fact that not only was I following her classes with great enthusiasm, but was doing so with considerable grace and flair. Fortunately, Mary Horwitz, one of the more established ballet-mums and an old friend of the family, took it upon herself to speak up on my behalf. 'Sheila', she said with frustration, 'it's high time you bought your own daughter some clothes befitting a ballet class. And some ballet shoes for goodness' sake.' My mother was clearly taken aback by her remark and, much to my delight, I didn't have to wait long before Mary's plea was answered.

'Good morning Miss Wartski', a middle aged lady said politely, as we entered Johannesburg's main ballet provision store. 'I haven't seen you for a while. What can I do for you today?' Then came the reply for which I had been waiting for so long - music to my ears. 'I've come to buy a pair of pink satin ballet shoes for my daughter Clair'. Looking down at my small feet, Mrs. Williams said hesitantly, 'Hmm, about size ten I would think. Take a seat please'. She ushered us towards two leather chairs before disappearing through a door to the back of the shop. It seemed an interminably long time before she reappeared. Carrying a few small grey boxes under her right arm, I looked on as she delicately unfolded some tissue paper revealing what seemed to me a treasure trove - the most exquisite pair of sparkling satin ballet shoes ever manufactured. I was breathless as she gently slipped them onto my feet. 'Stand on this rug and point your toes please Clair so I can see the fit'. I stood and pointed as requested, but my mind was already made up - I knew that I never wanted to take them off again. 'Mum, they are so comfortable, I don't need to try on any more pairs. They are perfect.' 'Well', my mother said, her tone business like and matter-of-fact, 'they do look the right size for you now, although there is not much growing room. Never mind', she decided quickly, 'we'll take them'. When we walked out of that wonderful shop, my favourite in the whole of Johannesburg, I was the proud owner of a black leotard, tights large enough to wrinkle at my knees, and those beautifully stitched ballet shoes, with the manufacturer's name Frederick Freed delicately engraved into their leathery soles. Later my mother showed me how to wind the soft ribbons around my ankles and tie them into a secure knot, discreetly placed on the inside of my leg. It seemed as if I had been given an official permit to enter into the world of classical ballet. Little did I know that I would spend the best part of the next four decades as a ballet dancer. But on that particular day in October 1959 my dream had come true and I glowed with pride, basking in the sensation of feeling like a proper ballerina.

It was not my mother's style to call out an alphabetic list of names in class. She was far too busy for that. But had she done so a typical register would have read something like this: Cohen, De Toit, Feldman, Getz, Goldschmidt, Gottleib, Jacobson, Janks, Lipschitz, Lubinsky, Oken, Shevitz, Van der Merwe and Zuckerman. No degree in social anthropology is required to see that though there were a couple of typically Afrikaner names, the vast majority of pupils attending the Sheila Wartski Academy of Dance were, like my mother, of good South African Jewish stock, their predecessors almost all from Lithuania, in keeping with the greater part of South African Jewry.

While the majority of Johannesburg's Jews would quietly inform you over dinner that racial prejudice was abhorrent to Judaism and that because discrimination was indivisible it was a Jewish obligation to oppose apartheid, they did not act on such fine sentiments. Some actively supported the National Party, even putting themselves forward as candidates, but most simply got on with their lives, my own family included. In so doing we all turned a blind eye to the most blatant of injustices played out before us, and thus validated apartheid.

And yet a minority did not. Although South Africa's Jews made up less than half of one per cent of the country's population, when 150 political leaders were arrested and charged with high treason in December 1956 - Mandela included - more than half of the whites arrested were Jews. Opposition to apartheid was closer to home than I knew at the time. Elaine Gottleib - the mother of my best friend and fellow dance pupil Sue - was a close confidante of no less a figure than Helen Suzman, who represented my family's Houghton constituency. Sue's mother regularly hosted Suzman's Progressive Party gatherings in her elegant home on Houghton Ridge. The liberal Progressive Party's sole parliamentarian for many years and South Africa's only elected representative unequivocally opposed to apartheid, Suzman often slipped away from the comforts of Houghton to visit Nelson Mandela, who remained locked up on Robben Island. The rest of us, in our different ways, allowed him to languish there for more than a quarter of a century.

Did I understand the issues of apartheid? Hardly - I was a small child when the Treason Trials were underway and the political activities of my best friend's mother were a matter of supreme indifference to me. What was not a matter of indifference, however, was progress on my technique, the eisteddfods taking place in Jo'burg City Hall, the pleasure of taking additional classes in Spanish dance with Mercedes Melina or preparing for the latest end-of-year show at my mother's Academy. The annual performance was the occasion for parents to observe their offspring - some talented, some talentless - demonstrate dance routines on stage in a production performed by all the students of the ballet school. Colourful costumes, make up and music all contributed to the excitement and success of the day. At the end of the show, a large silver trophy would be awared to the pupil who had - in my mother's opinion - made the most progress during the course of the year. I would look on enviously as, year after year, the trophy would fall into everyone else's hands other than my own. I sensed that I was in for the long haul. Imagine my delight though when, one year, finally, my mother called out the name 'Clair Symonds' and I stepped forward to claim that trophy as my own.

It was all too easy to be lulled into thinking, in my native South Africa, that the worlds of art and apartheid were entirely unrelated. But in keeping with virtually every other aspect of daily life, they were in fact closely intertwined, as my family would in due course discover.

The recruiting grounds of my mother's dance studio were the privileged white suburbs of Johannesburg, and Jewish Johannesburg at that, but this didn't prevent her from deciding it would be a good idea to teach in the run-down, segregated and so-called 'coloured' township of Coronationville.

Sister Anunciata, the head of Coronationville's Saint Theresa Convent School, had heard of my mother's growing reputation and approached her to see if she would consider teaching ballet to her pupils.

'Definitely', she informed her, without a moment's hesitation. 'A child is a child, no matter what the colour of her skin', she insisted to my father. 'They all deserve a chance'. Such an assertion might sound rather pedestrian now but in the South Africa of the 1960s it was close to revolutionary.

In the complex jargon of apartheid and the bizarre vocabulary it spawned, the term coloured referred to an ethnic group possessing sub-Saharan ancestry but not in sufficient quantity to be considered black under the law. The Group Areas Act had seen to it that different races were assigned their own residential and business areas, not just in Johannesburg but throughout the country. For a white person to enter an area set aside for those of mixed race required police permission, and a secondary permit in my mother's case since she intended to work there. Her self-imposed brief was as far from the political as one can imagine - teaching ballet to a few dozen schoolchildren classified by Pretoria as mixed race.

This was how I too came to meet Sister Anunciata. She oversaw the teaching of around four hundred young girls and ran her school under the auspices of the diocese of Johannesburg, whose motto, 'For God, in Peace and Joy', belied the rigid framework of apartheid. Sister Anunciata was delighted to be able to add ballet to the school's curriculum and welcomed my mother with great enthusiasm. But this was no flash-in-the-pan charitable endeavour on my mother's part - she spent sixteen years training and coaching the convent children of Coronationville. I stood uncomfortably by her side in front of a classroom of children not much younger than myself as they rose from their seats to chant in unison 'Good morning Miss Sheila,' and then, to my eternal embarrassment, an equally loud and impeccably delivered chorus of 'Good morning Miss Clair.' The machinery of apartheid was nothing if not efficient, and I realised that I had never before been to an area where non-white people lived or went about their business.

I sat feeling somewhat awkward and out of place on a small wooden chair in front of the class of eight or more 'coloured' boys and girls. I watched my mother as she got into her stride - 'let's do *pliés* followed by *tendues*', 'point your toes Jacob', 'Ginny, a little more incline of your head, please', 'good poise Sookie'. Criticisms and praise in equal measure, their smiles and laughter at my mother's humorous remarks lifting everyone's spirits, the allotted hour going by in a flash. I began to understand that when it came to dance my mother was entirely colour-blind, the complex racial politics of apartheid positively the last thing on her mind. Even Mrs. Malamade was brought along to thump away at the piano.

As my mother's reputation as one of Johannesburg's premier teachers of dance continued to grow, she was now actively sought out by producers to work as a choreographer in her own right, opportunities she seized and carried out with characteristic originality and flair. I would accompany her as she set about finding authentic dancers to participate in all-black musicals and African films and watched enthralled as she arranged traditional set-piece Zulu mine dances and worked alongside tribesmen and native peoples in the most remote corners of South Africa's flat and sparsely populated scrubland known as the *karoo*.

From coloured townships to the recording of the film *Dingaka* - now in my teens - I looked on as my mother's world began to spiral more and more into non-white territory. Of course her remit was related to choreography and artistic direction, but the message of the acclaimed Afrikaner writer-producer Jamie Uys was not difficult to decode. *Dingaka* was the story of an African tribesman seeking revenge against the people who murdered his daughter and whose crusade leads him into the white man's courts. It was all part and parcel of the many contradictions of apartheid South Africa where the arts flourished and an independent judiciary likewise thrived. But it was extremely dangerous territory.

It came as a relief to my father when, having completed her various film projects, my mother returned to her more traditional domain, creating the Sheila Wartski Dance Theatre Group, the heart and administrative soul of which was her home-based studio in trouble-free white suburbia. It was very much a family affair - my father putting his engineering skills to good use by designing and constructing the props while my brother Michael, five years my senior, helped out with the lighting, sound and stage management. For my father it seemed like a welcome return to normality - that was until

Philip Golding strode into the studio. With a worn out grey dance bag thrown casually over his shoulder, he announced that he had studied movement in his native London and was keen to join the company. My mother's prayers were answered: finally, a male dancer, for up until that point the company had consisted of fifteen of us girls but just one boy - an awkward, dark haired young man named Ranan Lubinsky. My own prayers seemed to have been answered too - here was a good-looking young man in his early twenties with an attractive physique and an appealing English accent. But it soon became clear I would have to take my place in the queue since the entire female contingent of the company had their eye on the new arrival. Philip would in due course prove himself to be a consistently hard worker.

His curly hair and sharp brown eyes emphasised a well structured jaw-line and unshaven face, his flirting and cheekiness part and parcel of his many winning ways. He soon became an integral part of our small but determined group of dancers, all of whom would sacrifice evenings and weekends to rehearse for upcoming performances. It was a relief to see that he had some dance training too with a technique good enough for my mother's stringent requirements and he was - to her evident delight - a surprisingly strong *pas-de-deux* partner, allowing her to open up a new dimension of innovative choreography for the company. Aware that Philip was alone, having not long arrived in South Africa, my mother would invite him to dine with us from time to time. It was during these more intimate occasions that we came to understand that as flamboyant as Philip might have been within the structure of the company and studio walls, so he was reticent to talk of his life outside of the troupe, giving little to nothing away.

Then, as though the sun was shining down on our studio, another man came knocking on our door. He introduced himself as Jan du Plessis. In a strong Afrikaner accent - such a contrast to the rakish Philip - he got straight to the point: 'I want to learn to dance.' Here was a most unlikely ballet pupil. My mother looked at the gangly six foot man staring down at her and tried to work out where on earth he might fit in. 'Actually, I would like to have private lessons,' he added, sensing my mother's bemusement. 'Oh, that's fine,' she replied. 'There's a half-hour slot free on Friday mornings.' 'I'll take it,' he said, rather too quickly.

Over the following months my mother, who had the reputation of being able to turn almost anyone into a dancer given sufficient time, was beginning to feel the strain. 'This man's got two left feet', she complained to my father. 'It beats me why he wants to dance at all.'

My father, never one to lavish sympathy, chuckled and mumbled into his daily paper, 'you married me and I've got two left feet.'

My relentless drive to become a professional dancer appeared now to have taken on a momentum of its own. Every day, it seemed to me, my technique was gaining strength - a daily diet of vigorous classes saw to that. Disciplined and driven, I would run home from school, throw off my uniform and with it any thoughts of that morning's intellectual pursuits, homework included, and happily put on my tights, leotard and ballet shoes, impatient for the demanding afternoon class to begin. The piano music inspired me to ignore any aching muscles, any pulling at the back of my thighs as I stretched to the floor and any tender toes as I hopped up and down on them willing potential blisters not to develop and claim their victory. I would happily anticipate the preparation of a leap that would send me flying through the air or feel the exhuberance of spinning across the studio floor, my arms held out firmly in front for balance, always focusing determinedly on my chosen direction, like an eagle eyeing its hapless prey.

Towards the end of the September of 1967, two public performances were scheduled to take place in the main hall at the Jabula Social Centre in Sandringham, a suburb to the north east of Johannesburg. With twenty one dancers and ballets ranging from Spirituals to the Roaring Twenties, rehearsals had reached fever pitch. But for me the undoubted highlight of our performances would always be her staging of Paul Galico's Snow Goose - the touching parable of friendship and eventual love of a young girl with a disabled artist who lived as a recluse in an abandoned light house in the marshlands of England. She had sensitively choreographed a contemporary ballet to nothing more elaborate than the haunting voice of the main character, Philip Rhayader. Her staging saw to it that there was rarely a dry eye in the house by the time the final curtain came down. Needless to say I was desperate to dance the main role - that of Fritha. But aged just fourteen the best my mother could come up with for me was the role of the Snow Goose itself, and even that was merely as a background shadow, although evidently nonetheless effective for that. Anxious to get the Thursday night dress rehearsal underway she was loudly venting her frustration that Philip Golding was late and as such was in no mood to notice Michael calling her to the phone. Could he not see that this was no time to take calls? 'Who is it?' she snapped, her mind focusing on the dancers positioning themselves for the opening of the show, as the overture got underway.

'Yes', she barked out, barely able to recognise Philip's voice. 'I've been arrested by the Security Police under the Terrorism Act,' he said shakily. 'This is the only call I'm allowed to make. I'm very sorry Sheila but I won't be able to make the rehearsal tonight or the performance on Friday.' The news from Philip struck like a bolt of lightening. Rapidly regaining her composure, my mother interrupted the rehearsal to inform the company of Philip's arrest. Despite the knowledge that the troupe and its members were now clearly within the radar of the secret police, my mother, ever the professional, went straight about the business of reorganising the gaps where Philip should have been dancing so that the performance at the social centre not be delayed. We were all perfectly well aware of the old showbiz cliché that the show had to go on. And it did.

My father had more earthly matters on his mind. Pieces of the jigsaw were beginning to fall into place, forming an uneasy and unsettling shape. Since Philip's departure, the half-hour slot on Friday mornings, so sought after by Jan du Plessis, was now available. He too had mysteriously disappeared. News filtered through that Philip had been accused of working for the outlawed African National Congress. The ANC was the main vehicle of political opposition to apartheid, albeit an illegal one. Although founded in 1912 it had only formally adopted its Freedom Charter in the 1950s, a document in which the movement's core principles were set out, with an inspirational rallying call for democracy and insistence that 'The People Shall Govern!' Small wonder that it should have been banned by the apartheid regime. In fact one of the 3000 delegates endorsing the Freedom Charter was Nelson Mandela, only managing to escape the police on that occasion by disguising himself as a milkman, his movements already restricted by a series of banning orders at that time.   At the other end of the political spectrum was BOSS, the much feared and ruthlessly efficient Bureau of State Security.   Of course he didn't go around sporting a badge to that effect, but my father became convinced that the company's second male recruit, the talentless and privately coached student Jan du Plessis, was a spy tracking Philip for that organisation.

Philip Golding in the ANC.   Jan du Plessis working for BOSS.   And both of them in and out of my mother's studio.   My father might not have had an active interest in politics but nor was any required for him to realise that it was all too close to home.   He smelled danger in the air.   He tried to convince my mother that our telephone was being tapped, citing evidence of a constant crackling on the line to back up his case.   A climate of fear and intimidation slowly began to cloud over our home in Houghton.   My father, proud to claim that he was born in Mare Street, Hackney - and thus within the sound of London's Bow Bells - concluded that his stay in South Africa, which had lasted nearly three decades, had now run its course.   I'd never seen him so resolute but I knew he would never gamble with the safety of his family.   Besides, the Cockney boy who went on to be educated at Haberdashers' Aske's Boys' School was not altogether displeased at the prospect of returning to England for his retirement. The writing was on the wall: it was time for us to pack our bags and leave South Africa.   It was a decision that happened to coincide with my own hopes and aspirations.

Chapter 4: Chester Close South, Regent's Park, London, 1970

Barely seventeen, I had little idea how much my lifestyle was about to change. London was far bigger than I imagined and our tiny two-bedroom flat at Chester Close South near Regent's Park was a stark contrast to the swimming pools and tennis courts of Johannesburg. But most surprising of all, and yet so easy to adapt to, was that in London I was part of a thriving multi-cultural society where members of different races and people of different colour could hold hands in public without fear of sanction, live in the same area as whites without violating any Group Areas Act and most importantly of all, enjoy full and equal rights before the law. I had always been told that the end of apartheid would mean the end of South Africa. I finally understood what that phrase meant: the end of *white* South Africa.

My mind was preoccupied with other matters though, most notably with my own good news: I had auditioned and been accepted at the Royal Ballet School, based in Barons Court - the offer of a scholarship the cherry on the cake. It felt as if I had been rewarded for the many years of training, the endless *pliés* and *tendues* and the often rather unforgiving regime of the Cecchetti ballet syllabus. As I celebrated my success I had little idea of the relentless battering my ego was about to undergo.

Taking my place at the *barre* along with the other young hopefuls, I had every reason to feel among equals. I glanced at the gifted dancers either side of me, all creamed off as future young hopefuls for the Royal Ballet, a world-class company with an unmatched repertoire and back-catalogue of productions, and thus potential rivals rather than class-mates. 'Two demi *pliés* and one *grande* followed by *porte de bras en avant*', came Miss Farron's instructions, jolting my mind back to the work at hand. 'And one *en arrière*', she continued. The kindly ballet mistress conducted the class with a generous attitude and perceptive eye. Over the coming weeks and months it became obvious that we were all being processed, in a sense, to acquire the requisite reserved 'look' of a dancer with potential for the Royal's *corps de ballet*. In my case this meant that old habits had to be broken - and fast.

'Lower your arms please Clair, they are far too grand and broad. That Russian style is not what the Company is after. We are looking for smaller, modest arm movements - please, bend them more into your body ... think of the reserve of *Les Sylphides*.' That struck a chord since that romantic *ballet blanc* had long been my favourite. Whatever the case it was clear the style which had become familiar to me had to go.

Because the Company and the School then shared premises and facilities it was not uncommon to cross paths with the legendary Margot Fonteyn and Rudolf Nureyev - considered by many balletomanes to be one of the greatest dancing partnerships of all time. It was of course enormously inspiring to be in their presence. But it could also be devastatingly crushing, at least in respect of the temperamental Tatar, who had defected to Paris some years earlier, despite the best efforts of the KGB to prevent him from doing precisely that. The buzz at Barons Court was that Nureyev was rehearsing in the main studio and, unusually, the door to it had been left wide open. It wasn't long before a small crowd of over-excited students, myself included, dashed down the long corridor leading to the main company rehearsal studio. The race was on. We elbowed, jockeyed and pushed one another out the way to gain the best position in the doorway in order to catch a glimpse of the great star himself.

In fact we were to get more than we bargained for. With the rehearsal evidently not going his way, he stormed out of the studio and headed straight for us. His eyes flashed with impatience, his Slavic face tense as he dismissed us with a grand gesture of his right arm, its position elegant and graceful despite his manifest anger. 'All of you,' he bellowed, 'clear off, go away - you're distracting us. Can't you see that we are trying to concentrate?' Contrary to all notions of training in classical ballet, we scampered away like naughty puppies in disgrace. Still, it was an enormous privilege to rub shoulders on my way to classes with the likes of Anthony Dowell and Antoinette Sibley - stars of the Royal Ballet I had come across thanks to my monthly *Ballerina* magazines in South Africa. It was the same story whilst rehearsing *La Fille Mal Gardée* in front of Sir Frederick Ashton, not only the original choreographer of that two-act comic ballet but the founder choreographer of the Royal Ballet itself. How my life had changed in such a short space of time. Compared to Johannesburg where I had won numerous awards for ballet and was part of the fixtures and fittings when it came to dance festivals, I had now become a very small fish in an extremely deep and prestigious pond.

During the course of my training at the Royal Ballet School, my mother - who had always been responsible for overseeing my development as a dancer - had been frustrated at the lack of opportunity to observe my progress. So she was delighted when an invitation dropped through the letter box of our small two-bedroomed apartment near Regent's Park inviting parents to attend the annual demonstration class scheduled to take place in a hall near Primrose Hill. Rehearsals in this new environment had proved to be rather fraught because the grand studio there had a very shiny and heavily waxed wooden floor - lethal for ballet dancers - and thus clearly an inappropriate choice of venue. No matter how much resin we crunched under our ballet shoes in an attempt to provide grip, the floor remained slippery, our feet unsteady. The formidable Miss Fewster, the School's principal, who let it be known that she would be attending the demonstration, insisted that she would only allow her students to dance if they had rubber soles fitted to their shoes.

Unused to the restraint of the rubber sole, we now found ourselves confronting the opposite dilemma - almost sticking to the floor. The demonstration was an unmitigated disaster. And now to face my mother - who always gave me her honest opinion. She hadn't seen me dance since leaving South Africa and she was uncharacteristically quiet on the car ride home, which served only to make the wait more uncomfortable. Eventually it came out. As I knew it would. 'Oh my God, Clair. What have they done to you?'

In South Africa I had never given much thought to the issue of weight, but in London I was suddenly challenged with it. Unused to stodgy English fare, I was fast becoming a chubby 17-year-old and nowhere was my new size more apparent than in the school's changing rooms where I was faced with an endless stream of skinny, flat-chested students parading the 'perfect' ballet dancer's physique. My now ample bosom didn't fit the required look. It might not have been written on the school's curriculum but everyone knew that big boobs and ballet dancers don't go together. So, with the help of a pair of tights stretched almost to breaking point and a black cross-over top, I managed to flatten my bust and regain a measure of my former confidence.

But that soon proved to be short-lived. As the end of the second and final year of school approached in the late spring of 1972, I was summonsed to the Ballet Principal's office. Miss Fewster had joined the Sadler's Wells Ballet School in 1942 at the age of 14 and her austere manner had always terrified me. With her straight brown hair tied in a bun at the nape of her neck, she marched around the school's premises scrutinising the activities in every studio en route, provoking undiluted fear among her fragile young recruits. My heart pounding, I braced myself for her evaluation: Judgment Day had arrived.

'Please do sit down,' she began courteously. Her message was brief and to the point. 'Having consulted with a number of teachers, I have regretfully come to the conclusion that your style of dance is not at all conducive to a career in the Company. It is far too Russian and not at all what we are looking for.' I sat stiffly facing Miss Fewster wondering if she could actually hear the loud pounding of my heart. I knew that it would be courteous to reply, but my throat went dry and all that I could manage was an embarrassingly croaky 'oh'. Then, with an unusual softening in her demeanour, she continued 'I really am very sorry Clair...' Clair? I was surprised that she knew my name, for in the two years of training she had barely laid eyes on me let alone referred to me by name. Miss Fewster must have seen it all thousands of times before as she delivered her career-breaking blows. As my eyes misted over in an unsuccessful attempt to conceal my disappointment, she continued with her verbal onslaught. 'But I would like to take this opportunity of wishing you the very best of success elsewhere. I know that most of our students are readily accepted into other ballet companies.' I mustered up the little courage required to thank her for her time and left the frosty atmosphere of her office.

Miss Fewster's pronouncement came as a severe blow. To make matters worse, I was acutely aware that the end of the school year was only a few weeks away. I left her office despondent and numbed with the sadness of what might have been. 'Too Russian indeed', my mother muttered contemptuously upon learning of my bad news. 'Can't they appreciate that the openness of the Russian style is one of the greatest gifts ever brought to the world of classical ballet?' Still, we both had to get over it. In the event my recovery from rejection happened more rapidly than I could ever have imagined. For the following morning I was back at Barons Court making my way to the school's spacious changing rooms when I heard my name echoing through the long walkways. Turning round, I noticed Miss Farron waving to me. Julia Farron had been the very first scholarship pupil at the Ninette de Valois' school after its establishment at Sadler's Wells Theatre in the 1930s. She had been an immensely effective and sympathetic teacher during my first year. Having gone on to become principal dancer at the Royal Ballet - she had a lifetime's experience in the performing arts.

'I am so glad you're here Clair,' she said. 'I was hoping to catch you. Get yourself changed right away and come and join my lesson. It's an audition class for a ballet company. They're looking for two dancers.' I'd spent countless hours in ballet studios - years if you totted them up. And all for what? To dance professionally in a ballet company. Having recently experienced the bitter taste of rejection, I had no intention of letting this opportunity pass me by.

The class was held in front of Anne Heaton, a woman in her mid-thirties, whose dark hair and heavy make up accentuated her brown eyes. She sat next to a middle-aged man whose plump hands rested on his protruding belly. Every so often I noticed their whispering together while focusing on one student or another - each dancer hoping it would be them. I decided that this time I wasn't going to give up without a fight. From the very first *plié* to the final curtsy of the class, I danced as if it were a performance in front of a packed house on the stage of the Royal Opera House itself.

Everything seemed to fall into place. My *arabesques* were held for that much longer, my pointed feet beat that much sharper, *developées* seemed that much lighter, *grandes jeteés* hovered a touch higher until, finally, I *chainé*'d my way effortlessly towards my goal - the undivided attention of our guests.

It wasn't long before I found myself back in Miss Fewster's office. She introduced me to Mr.Nejad Ahmadzadeh, director of the Iranian National Ballet Company, the portly man who had flown over from Tehran to select his new recruits. I couldn't hold back a triumphant smile as they both held out their hands to congratulate me. Two Royal Ballet School students had been selected - Karen Oram and myself. Up until that audition we had been in different classes, having little to do with one another. But now, it seemed, our respective fates were poised to become intertwined.

When I arrived home my parents, seeing my cheerful demeanour, were puzzled as to what might have happened to turn my fortunes around in such a short space of time. 'Iran,' my mother exclaimed. 'Where on earth is Iran?' Before long an assortment of encyclopaedias, atlases and reference books were piled up on the carpet of our living room. My father was anxious to get down to the practicalities. 'And did this Mr. Midziday . . .' 'Ahmadzadeh - daddy,' I interrupted. 'Yes,' he said, clearing his throat, '. . . and did he offer you a contract for your employment out there?' That was an easy one to answer. 'No, he did not.'

The very next day my mother contacted an official from Equity, the London-based trade union representing the interests of professional performers. She needed to know if they would offer me protection while I was in Iran. At their headquarters in Harley Street a middle-aged Equity official invited us into his plush office. With a businesslike half-smile, he sat behind a pile of papers neatly stacked on his desk. It must have been on his mind because he mentioned, unprompted, that he was actively involved with Equity's 'Living Wage' campaign which had set a target of £18 as a minimum weekly wage for its members. Such preoccupations had evidently not prevented him from doing his homework in respect of my own case. He immediately placed another set of papers on his desk - evidence, he explained. They were letters from distraught parents who had flown all the way to Tehran to collect their disenchanted offspring from one particular institution - the Iranian National Ballet Company. It was hardly the promising start I'd been hoping for. His message couldn't have been more clear - avoid Iran at all costs.

'But, please, do allow me to take a closer look at your contract,' he continued. 'I haven't received one yet,' I mumbled with shrinking conviction. 'What?', he exclaimed, placing his hand on his forehead and leaned forward slightly, unable to conceal his despair. 'And just when do you expect to get one?' I repeated what Mr. Ahmadzadeh had told me, that I would be able to inspect the document upon arrival in Tehran. This naïve revelation served only to enrage the Equity official further. 'Don't you realise that every single term and condition of that contract will be written in Farsi? You won't understand a single word of it. By which time it will almost certainly be too late. I'm very sorry Miss Symonds,' he added in the regretful tone of someone about to break bad news, 'but Equity will be unable to provide you with any protection whatsoever.'

I'm not sure if he took pity on me, perhaps he saw how desperately I wanted the job, but suddenly his tone softened. 'Miss Symonds... Clair, listen to me. Do you know how difficult it is to obtain an Equity card?' Of course I knew, the students of the Royal Ballet School talked of little else. 'Well,' he said as though he was about to play a concealed trump card. 'If you don't go to Tehran I will personally see to it that you receive full Equity membership within a few weeks.'

As my mother and I left Equity's West End offices we walked home in silence. Shortly after arriving at our flat the phone rang. It was Miss Fewster, asking if I had made up my mind. Mr. Ahmadzadeh was due to return to Iran and needed an answer. 'My parents are very worried. They think I may be making a rather hasty decision'. 'There have been problems with foreign dancers, that is true', she replied. 'But that was all many years ago and recently the company has made great strides. The Royal Ballet School would never contemplate sending dancers out there if that were not the case.' That was sufficient for me to make up my mind. 'I'm going to do it, Miss Fewster. I'm going to join the Iranian National Ballet!'

'Would you fasten your seat belts, please, the Captain has now begun his descent'. The voice over the aircraft's tannoy was slightly accented, but the message perfectly clear.   With its human cargo of some three hundred passengers, we were now beginning what appeared to be a rather rapid descent towards the largest conglomeration in the whole of the Middle East - the sprawling city of Tehran.

Chapter 5: The Vibrancy of Tehran

It was July. Which was why, as soon as the aeroplane door opened, we were overwhelmed by the stifling heat of Tehran. In a display of typically warm Iranian hospitality, the director of the ballet company Mr. Ahmadzadeh, together with his striking wife Aida, had made the short trip out to Mehrabad airport to personally welcome his new arrivals from London - an unlikely assortment of dancers, musicians, teachers and choreographers. It was something of a relief to board the air-conditioned coach he had kindly organised to take us to the city centre and an even greater relief when we pulled up in front of our stylish destination - the flashy five-star Tehran Hilton, its ostentatious foyer dripping in marble and lavishly decorated with exquisitely-woven Persian carpets. There the director ushered us together and gave a brief welcoming speech. Staring out from beneath thick, bushy eyebrows, he scrutinised the new intake before announcing that classes would begin in exactly one week. I wondered how many of us had been personally selected by Mr. Ahmadzadeh. I knew that the Royal Ballet School had provided just two - Karen Oram and me. His Iranian accent was far more pronounced than I could recall from the auditions at Barons Court. 'Between now and then, you will be expected to find yourselves suitable living accommodation - and try to make sure it is not too far from Talar Roudaki, the theatre where we are based.' Considering English was not his mother tongue, he managed to get his next message across rather succinctly - that once rehearsals had got underway we were all more than welcome to stay on at the hotel. But that it would henceforth be at our own expense, information which succeeded in rapidly concentrating minds and wiping the smiles off our faces.

There then followed an unseemly dash towards the hotel's large swimming pool, set in spacious lawns. As I sunbathed on the teak loungers scattered liberally around the poolside, sipping chilled drinks and getting to know fellow company members - I arrived at what was, admittedly, a rather hasty preliminary conclusion - that Iran really wasn't that bad after all. So much for those scaremongers back home, so ready to dish out their depressing prophesies of doom and gloom.

It was not that Karen and I came to be bored with the good life provided courtesy of the Tehran Hilton. Not at all. Although impatient to leave the confines of the luxurious hotel, we set off on foot towards the city centre with a sense of trepidation and unease. This was almost entirely attributable to the reckless driving all around us, which gave rise to an ever-present but not ill-founded fear of being run-over or crushed, possibly even both, one's presence on the pavement notwithstanding. Hands on horns, the over-excited drivers whose cars constituted the terrible traffic of Tehran would recklessly switch from one lane to another with little or no regard for other vehicles, swearing and gesticulating as they did so and always jockeying for pole position at traffic lights, where we would nervously wait to cross the road. I felt some pity for the lone traffic policeman I glimpsed, whistle in mouth, standing vulnerably on his small central platform but being afforded only grudging acknowledgement, if indeed any at all, his arms flailing in every direction in an apparently hopeless battle against the surrounding chaos. And scattered liberally throughout the city the pampered and privileged, the well-heeled and well-connected but also the blind and disabled, the homeless and dispossessed, breathing in, as we all were, poisonous exhaust fumes belching out from barely road-worthy vehicles clogging the city's poorly-designed network of pot-holed roads.

'Misses, please. You want I sell you English newspaper or maybe packet of sunflower seeds?' We turned round to see an elderly man, of slender frame and slightly stooped, standing protectively by his modest stall - one of the countless street corner traders of Tehran. His baggy trousers were faded and threadbare. He stretched out a thin hand in our direction. 'No want to buy?' Sensing our lack of interest, he immediately tried another tack, shouting out 'come here, have very good cold fruit juice or maybe ice-cream - not like your ice-cream, good Iran ice-cream.' Doing our utmost to cope with the blistering heat, we sat on a weather-beaten wooden bench and for a brief moment cut off from the whirlwind of street life in the Iranian capital. Having succumbed rather readily to the sales patter of the street vendor, we allowed the subtle aroma of rose-scented ice-cream to cool our parched throats and revive our flagging spirits. I closed my eyes for just a few moments. Suddenly I heard Karen calling out my name. I sat bolt upright, taking hold of her arm. 'What is it?'

'Look up'. I stared right into her eyes. 'No, I mean look up there', pointing impatiently to the sky. The intensity of the daylight made me squint for a few moments, but I soon began to focus on the snow-capped mountains to the north of Tehran. It was my first glimpse of the majestic Alborz Mountains. Stretching from the borders of Armenia right down to the Caspian Sea, they provided a picturesque frame and welcome calming presence to Tehran, in addition to a constant supply of water to the city centre and beyond via a network of wide gutters known as jubes.

We continued on our way with renewed energy. Tehran was teeming with life and we were happy to be part of it. Elegant, olive-skinned women sat outside cafés chatting animatedly over cups of Turkish coffee. Some were dressed in chic European designs, Vuitton handbags casually placed on their laps and it was by no means rare to catch a whiff of the exclusive aromas of Chanel or Dior in the air. Other women had opted for the modesty and discretion of the *chador*, covering their bodies head-to-toe in a full-length semicircle of fabric that appeared to have no hand openings or closures at all. And yet their long flowing garments seemed not to impede upon daily life in any way. Even a take-your-life-in-your-hands dash to cross the streets appeared to be simplicity itself -often with children and buggies in tow. A confusing mixture of modernity and the traditional, the pace of life in the Iranian capital was exhilarating and exhausting at the same time. Taxis being hailed, women carrying baskets over flowing with fruit and vegetables or fresh cuts of meat from the market, older men sitting peacefully - their eyes often glazed over from smoking hubbly bubbly - some of them rolling dice, as if their lives depended on it, in an intense game of back-gammon. But the mouth-watering smell of *chelo kebab* wafting in our direction from a local restaurant was the one temptation to which we all too readily succumbed - the first of many encounters with the delicious national dish of Iran: we eagerly devoured the barbequed minced lamb served with lashings of buttered basmati rice and, despite our loud protestations to the contrary, the yolk of a raw egg thrown in.

Of course the chatter all around was as incomprehensible as the street names and signs above the shops, all written in Farsi, Iran's ancient official language. That was only to be expected. What was more difficult to cope with, though, as we continued exploring the city during our first few days in Iran was the undeniable reality that we were being stared at. Not a stolen glance here and there, which we might in ordinary circumstances have appreciated, but unrestrained, unrelenting and unsubtle staring in our direction. The interplay between the sexes was hardly a complex process to unravel or decode - young unaccompanied foreign girls were viewed as being of dubious moral character, easy pickings to be more precise, and evidently all the more attractive because of that. No doubt we should have seen them coming. But we did not. Two gangly teenagers, no more than fifteen years old, deliberately walked in our way, taking advantage of an accidently-on-purpose collision to grope at and fondle our bodies for a few illicit seconds. We stood in disbelief and shock before turning to go after them. We might have been fit young ballet professionals but they were soon well ahead, disappearing into the crowd. Irritated by such blatant sexual harassment, we headed back towards the security of the Hilton which, suddenly, seemed to acquire an even more attractive allure.

Ever since our successful audition at the Royal Ballet School, Karen and I had hardly been apart. During our first few weeks in Iran we had found comfort and security in our new friendship and because of that never really discussed the merits of sharing a flat together on the grounds that we both just assumed we would. In this respect good fortune was on our side. Anne Heaton, the vibrant and colourful choreographer whom we had first met at the audition at the Royal Ballet School in London, was about to move out of an apartment for something a little more up-market and had offered us first refusal on it. Just a short ten minute walk from Talar Roudaki, we were delighted that it had fallen into our laps so easily and set about occupying the top floor of a well-maintained old house in a relatively quiet back street of Tehran. The owners, an elderly Iranian couple, had converted it into a separate one-bedroomed apartment with a view to supplementing their retirement income. Although the brown tiled floor was spotless and punctuated with slightly faded Persian rugs, the heavy wooden furniture set out in the spacious living room seemed rather out of character with a large modern television perched on top of a chest of drawers. But the flat was affordable and its location ideal - close to a small local supermarket and in easy reach of other young dancers who, like us, has recently arrived in Tehran. The high ceilinged apartment, with its neutrally coloured papered walls and small kitchen, soon came to represent a cosy base from which we would be able to navigate our way through the tapestry of exciting new sights and sounds the Iranian capital offered in an apparently endless supply. Many mornings we would be woken by street vendors loudly declaring the merits of the wares stacked chaotically on the backs of donkey carts, on other occasions our sleep would be interrupted by melodious and oft-repeated chants of *allah akbar*, calling the Muslim faithful to prayer, a rallying call synonomous with the Middle East.

Apart from the business of paying our rent at the beginning of every month, Karen and I had little contact with our landlord or his wife or indeed any of the neighbours. We were young European girls, unable to read or understand even a single word of Farsi, entirely out of sync with the mind-set of the local population who, not unreasonably perhaps, must have come to wonder what such vulnerable youngsters were doing so far from the more certain and stable terrains of their own family homes.

Still, after just a few weeks in Iran I was missing my family enormously. Home-sickness was coming close to overwhelming me. Experiencing Iranian culture was fascinating, but at the same time had succeeded in turning my world upside down. I had grown up happily in the southern hemisphere before making a relatively painless transition to England in the rich north. But the ways of Iran and the east mystified me and I felt an urgent need to take strength from my family in London. When I phoned home I went out of my way to put on a cheery voice. Not that it fooled my father.

'What's the matter darling?' he asked. I missed home far more than I could have imagined. And now, on hearing my father's reassuring voice, I suddenly felt terribly exposed, like a vulnerable child. I poured out my heart.

'Dad, I want to give a month's notice,' I said a little shakily. 'I would like to leave Iran and come back to London.' I'd been mulling it over the previous evening.

Gathering his thoughts and reflecting quickly on my unexpected emotional outburst, my father stated his opinion. It wasn't what I wanted to hear. 'Clair, you know how much I would love you to come home. It's so quiet here and not the same without you. We miss you too - there's nothing that I would love more than to see you again. The sooner the better. But you've only been away for a few weeks, darling. It's such early days and you haven't really given yourself a chance. If you were to take my advice, I would say stick to it a little longer. If, after a few months, you still feel the same way, then I promise I will pay for your ticket back to London. Oh, and by the way, what's happened with your contract, have they come up with one and, if so, have you signed it yet?'

Goodness me, how to respond to that one? How to inform my father that I had put my signature to a legal document, but in circumstances precisely as predicted by the gentleman from Equity in London. How to tell him the truth - that I hadn't understood a single word of the beautifully written but entirely incomprehensible Iranian script which had been placed before me in Mr. Ahmadzadeh's office. I decided to spare myself any further embarrassment by replying to my father that, yes, the contract had been forthcoming and had indeed been signed.

'Then Clair, listen to me, now that you have committed yourself, it's just for one year, after all, then you should at least try and see it through'.

I knew my father's advice was sound and that I would have to learn to accept my new experiences and perhaps, one day, even to embrace them. It was a bitter pill to swallow – precisely the opposite of what I had wanted to hear. A year in Iran - how on earth would I cope?

Chapter 6: Talar Roudaki

When it came to the international pecking order of ballet companies, one hesitated to mention the Iranian National Ballet Company and the Royal Ballet in the same breath. Not so, however, when it came to monetary matters, for the company in Tehran was positively awash with funds.

I soon discovered why. Farah Pahlavi, the Empress of Iran or the Shahbanou as she was popularly known, had a habit of using her husband's influence to secure funding for causes close to her heart: women's rights - an innovative concept when it came to the Middle East - but at the very top of her agenda - the arts. She pulled strings at the Ministry of Culture and Arts on behalf of the Tehran Museum of Contemporary Art. But she pulled them still harder and more effectively for the National Ballet, of which she was patron. It was partly thanks to her initiative that the ballet company was created in the first place, five years prior to my arrival. Initially it had only a dozen or so dancers on the payroll, but by the time I stepped off the plane in Tehran its ranks had swollen to more than 40, two-thirds of whom were Iranian nationals. I learned that this was the way Iran functioned - there were scarcely any activities or vocations in which the Shah or members of his extended family or friends did not have a direct or symbolic involvement.

Talar Roudaki was quite some place of work. The newly-constructed home of the ballet company was built to celebrate the Shah's 'white revolution', a package of social and economic reforms designed to transform Iran into a global power. The building doubled as Iran's premier opera house and concert hall and was equipped with the latest technology. Named after the blind 10th-century poet Roudaki, the first great classical poet of Iran, the hall seated up to 1,600 people, its floodlit marble foyer incorporating an elegantly crafted traditional Talar motif, the Islamic equivalent to the Chinese moon gate. When I walked on to the stage for the first time and looked out towards where the audience would be seated, I was overwhelmed by the beauty of the white, gold and red décor so effectively recreating the luxurious atmosphere of established European opera houses with two tiers of boxes and a gallery overlooking the stalls.

It was the fourth floor of this modern complex which served as the hub of my ballet world in Tehran.   Aida Ahmadzadeh, the wife of our director Nejad, had been the first person to welcome us to our new work-place.   In her mid thirties, with a fine bone structure to which ample lashings of make up had been applied, she also happened to be one of the company's prima ballerinas.   In impeccable English she introduced us to existing company members, a large group of high-spirited young people chatting away in Farsi, but with more than the occasional phrase or two of English thrown in.   'Don't worry', she reassured us, 'most of us speak some English and we always work in that language. Maggie will show you where the girls' changing rooms are'.   Fresh faced and fair-skinned, Maggie Saghabashi was a pretty British ex-patriot who had married Jamshid, one of the leading Iranian dancers.   With the confident air of one who knew the local ropes, she marched us off to inspect the spacious changing rooms and the social area where dancers and teachers mingled and smoked or drank coffee and Coca-Cola after class.

It wasn't difficult to notice the Company's leading light.   Haydeh Hashemian's high cheek bones and brown eyes complimented her soft dark skin.   Although self-obsessed and ruthlessly ambitious, she was a proud and beautiful dancer, with a strong classical technique acquired in the Soviet Union.   When it came to the issue of casting, this could hardly be described as a fraught decision-making process: most of the lead roles were hers.   So when the list for the ballet *Scheherazade* was posted on the wall in the social room,   no one was in any doubt as to who the leading lady was likely to be. The ballet told the story of the legendary Persian queen and storyteller of *One Thousand and One Nights*, our production requiring the presence of six female slaves.   I was to be one of them, my flat-mate Karen too.   Still, I had been impatient to dance professionally and, as I would repeat to myself from time to time, things could only improve from the lowly world of slavery.

Just as speaking to my father a few weeks earlier had been the beginning of a turning point for me, so the pace of work at Talar Rudaki had quickened and I soon found myself being given more demanding roles.   I came to understand that little escaped the fastidious eye of Aida and I realised that she was behind my sudden and unexpected promotion first to a 'friend' in *Giselle* and then, to my astonishment, as a soloist in *Les Sylphides*. Respectable roles in two of the great ballet classics, it was a pleasure to finally be focusing on my work. That, after all, was the reason I had set off to Iran.

Ballet was my life. But I also loved the banter and back-chat when preparing for our usual morning class. 'Oh, shit, has anyone seen my right ballet shoe which has mysteriously gone missing', came a desperate cry from Gita, as we embarked upon a frantic search of the dressing-room. 'Check out the cupboard, Gita', Maggie replied, putting her hair effortlessly into a stylish chignon. 'There are often spare shoes in there.' 'Anyone got a few grips please?', I enquired, hoping that I was speaking loudly enough to counter the general chatter in the small changing room. 'I just need a couple to hold back my fringe!' 'Here you go curly', said another English dancer by the name of Ros, 'take the packet, keep them, as a present from me! Well from Amin actually', she added, instantly regretting having spilled the beans. 'Okay, so he bought me a packet of grips the other day when we were out for a snack lunch'. I looked at Ros, my eyebrows raised and grinning broadly. 'I knew the secret wouldn't last long' she said, 'we are seeing a lot more of each other outside of work'. I was thrilled for her. Amin was an engaging character, rather good looking and a talented dancer, one of the few male Iranian soloists in the company. Another English dancer, Marion, had no time for idle gossip, at least not then. 'Just off for a quick ciggie - see you in the studio', and she rushed off to the sitting area, where smoking was permitted, anxious for a quick fix of nicotine before the beginning of our strenuous exercises together.

A few minutes before the start of the lesson, Ros and I stood together in the resin box, inelegantly crunching our ballet shoes on the white sticky substance with a view to acquiring a good grip of the floor. 'Let's get together tonight for *chelo kebab*', I suggested. 'Sounds good to me, I'll check it out with Amin', and we proceeded to our usual places at the *barre*. In the far corner of the large mirrored studio, the pianist and conductor David Garforth, having adjusted the piano stool so that it was at the right height for him, sat surrounded by a wide selection of musical scores in preparation for the task ahead. A few minutes before 9 'o clock, the ballet-master Mr. Urazgildiev entered the studio and all nattering and chattering came to an abrupt end. Tall, well-built with strong slavic features and kindly blue eyes, his friendly smile belied the difficult class about to be inflicted upon company members. But we loved our Tatar trainer and knew even as the first exercise at the *barre* was getting underway, that our intrepid task-master would accept only work carried out to the best of our abilities. He would begin class with exercises designed to gradually stretch and warm up our bodies, toning and strengthening our muscles from feet and ankles right through to the upper arms and finger tips in the process. And when, inevitably, the strain would begin to show, inspiration would come from David Garforth's sensative renditions of Chopin, Bach or Mozart. After twenty minutes of rigorous *barre* work, we would move towards the centre of the room where equally challenging exercises designed to improve balance, strength and technical footwork would be followed by a series of pirouettes and energetic leaps from one side of the spacious studio to the other. No class would be complete without the traditional reverence or a balletic thank you to teacher and pianist alike, followed more often than not by spontaneous applause from us all - we, the assembled, exhausted but absolutely exhilirated members of the Iranian National Ballet.

My big break came far sooner than I could ever have imagined, although I rapidly discovered that there would be a price to pay for a new girl leaving the world of serfdom quite so speedily. Mr. Ahmadzadeh had given the green light to my understudying Haydeh Hashemian in her latest lead role. I thought there must have been a mistake as I spotted my name on the list. But there was not. And to make matters sweeter still, I was to be given a performance of my own - my first lead role in a major production. This time as Zarema, the King's erstwhile favourite within the royal harem in *The Fountain of Bakhchesarai* and, as the audiences at Talar Roudaki were poised to discover, possessed with the fiery temperment of a woman scorned.

In that respect I could see that the characters of the fictional Zarema and the real-life Haydeh shared common ground - especially when the lead of the Iranian ballet approached from behind and vented her wrath upon me. 'Just because you get to understudy me, don't think that you are a *prima ballerina*. You're still just a first year dancer here - a jumped up new girl. You'll never be as good as me ...'

I was flabbergasted. I knew perfectly well that ballet and bitchiness often went hand in hand - I had seen that in Johannesburg and London alike. But never before had I experienced such vitriol and venom. My retort was typically weak. 'I'm just doing what is asked of me.'

Still, this was how I found myself within intimate range of no less a figure than the Tatar King Khan Girey, the leading male role in the ballet. Needless to say Khan Girey lived in a magnificent palace from where, to my delight, he would lavish considerable attention towards Zarema. But I was only too well aware that he was overwhelmed with affection for another character - Maria, a Polish woman of aristocratic ancestry. Seized with jealousy, I would rush towards her with a dagger. But she showed no sign of fear, as if prepared to embrace her final moment. Shaking with rage, I held the shining silver dagger in both hands then plunged it deep into her heart. Within moments she was dead. She deserved it as the woman who had come between me and my beloved Khan Girey. Ending Maria's life in such a brutal manner was an enormously satisfying experience.

In keeping with many of the great classical ballets, here was a story that could only end in tears - for me as well, alas, when executioners swiftly appeared to lead Zarema to her own fate. The King ordered that she be hurled from the top of a high cliff so that His Majesty could also savour the taste of revenge. With its powerful score by Boris Azafiev, interspersed with strident passages inspired by the original Pushkin poem, it was a wonderfully lavish production with a beautifully constructed stone fountain - the fountain of tears - and grandiose staircase gracing the vast stage of the Iranian National Ballet. A leading role in a professional ballet company and generous applause from an evidently enchanted audience - everything I had ever hoped for. I was thrilled to be on stage in Tehran.

Ros was not the only one who had developed feelings for a good-looking Iranian dancer. For within the confines of Talar Roudaki I too began to feel affectionate towards Khan Girey, the Tatar king who commanded my character's demise. Perhaps I had taken the role of Zarema too closely to heart, but I became increasingly impatient for our scenes together to get underway. An extravagant costume enhanced his regal demeanour, skilfully applied make-up complementing his aura of resolution and intensity.   Inspired by the charisma of my royal partner and swept along by the force of the orchestration, I relished such proximity to my king.   My light gasps as I felt his warm breath on my neck were clearly not part of the performance - there are no sounds in classical ballet after all other than those emanating from the orchestra.   Nor were my knees meant to weaken at his warm regard.

Embracing the role of Zarema so whole heartedly represented a roller coaster of emotions - perfect for performances.   But my excitement and elation were mostly directed towards the charming and handsome Iranian dancer given the royal role - Arash Alizadeh.   It was clear from the enthusiastic greetings he received from the more established members of the company that he was a very popular character indeed, invariably the centre of attention.   I remember the first time I set eyes upon him.   As he strode imperiously across the studio, I knew right away that he had been cast as king.   In one sweeping glance, his perceptive dark brown eyes had scanned the rehearsal room, acknowledging new recruits with a friendly smile. But soon - too soon - I saw a noisy group of friends encouraging him back to their fold, greedy for his company, hungry for his news, impatient for his light-hearted jokes.   Feelings which I would come to share.

Anxious not to disclose my hand, I resisted the urge of attempting to ingratiate myself with what was obviously the ballet company's in-crowd. In any event I considered that he was out of my league. Who could possibly challenge the beauty and exoticism of those exquisite Persian princesses, their classically sculpted faces and dark silky hair cleverly crafted into *chignons*?   Not I.   I did my utmost to divert my thoughts but my gaze would inevitably stray across the studio back towards Arash.

A few days later there he was at the front door of the modest first floor flat I shared with Karen - Khan Girey himself.   'Hello there,' he shouted up,   relieved that at last someone had answered. 'Sorry, have I disturbed you?' 'No, no, of course not', I replied, thinking of the untidy lounge and dirty plates I had failed to clear from dinner the previous evening.   This was hardly my finest hour either - I looked a mess.   'No, not at all Arash. It's really nice to see you', I insisted.   I cleared my throat in a vain effort to give it some depth. But every time I spoke, my voice seemed to climb a semi-tone higher. 'Oh, please, do come up.' As he climbed the single flight of steps, it suddenly dawned on me - he'd come to see Karen. Of course.

'Oh, I'm so sorry,' I said, trying to stall him at the foot of the stairwell. 'But Karen's not here at the moment. She's gone away for the weekend.' As he reached the top of the stairs, there was little chance of preventing him from coming into the apartment. 'That's alright,' he replied, his lips parting into a half smile. 'It's you I've come to see. If you don't mind, that is.'

It struck me as wholly extraordinary that Arash would even have noticed me, let alone take time out to visit when he must surely have had so many friends vying for his time and attention. I felt incredibly flattered. He followed me into the small kitchen where I had been preparing some toast and coffee for breakfast. Looking up at my unexpected visitor, I smiled shyly. 'See, there's more than enough for the two of us. Why don't you stay and we'll eat together?'

That was it. Zarema and I - we were both under his spell. He flashed his beautiful eyes in my direction and with the smallest of smiles sent a frisson of excitement through my body. Not that I was going to give my hand away - so I enquired instead about his background and training in dance. He explained that he was the eldest of five children. 'My father is a retired colonel in the Shah's army. He was born and brought up in a military family - there was no way he would ever allow his son to do ballet. So when I was old enough to stand up to him, in my late teens, I began taking lessons. I love dancing - you can't imagine how thrilled I was to be asked to dance the role of Khan Girey.' Then he surprised me by stating that he wasn't a full time member of the ballet company. I did my best to conceal my disappointment at the prospect of a part-time king. 'You see I am a student at Tehran University - repeating my final year in architecture'. That could only be good news, I thought, the dreary architecture of Tehran was certainly in need of urgent reappraisal.

'I'm doing my final year for the third time and I don't intend to finish my degree, at least not in the current political climate'. I was

47

intrigued. I might not have been a leading light within the world of South African academia, but even I had never repeated a single year. 'Why not?' I asked. He carried on speaking but his tone seemed more guarded, his eyes lacking their earlier sparkle.

He surprised me by expressing his contempt for the Shah and all that he stood for. 'I have no intention of doing two years compulsory military service for his corrupt regime', he stated. 'I'm sorry, Arash, but I don't quite get it. What's military service got to do with your degree?' 'Well, pretty much everything, Clair'. He explained that he would only ever be issued with a passport upon completion of his military service - which he had not the slightest intention of doing. 'I feel as though I am trapped in my own country', he complained. A feeling of imprisonment made all the more frustrating because he knew full well that his sisters would be issued with their passports without undue delay on the grounds that girls were not required to serve in the formidable Iranian military machine.

'But the Iranian people must love the Shah even if you don't', I said. 'I see his picture in every shop and virtually everywhere I go.'

'I'm afraid that the law obliges all shops and offices to display a picture of the Shah. Besides, no shopkeeper worth his salt would even contemplate failing to display what is considered as an overt sign of loyalty to his regime.'

Arash was right. The Shah of Iran, Mohammad Rezā Shāh Pahlavi, *Shahanshah* or King of Kings, *Aryame* or Light of the Aryans, was indeed the law of the land. He was on the verge of abolishing the multi-party system of government with a view to ruling through a one-party state under the *Rastakhiz* or Resurrection Party - his party, of course.

While most of his subjects lived in appalling poverty, His Imperial Majesty had recently splashed out on celebrations for the 2,500 year anniversary of the Iranian monarchy. Arash described in great detail how over $100 million had been spent on the construction of a tented city next to the ruins of Persepolis - the ceremonial capital of the Persian Empire during the Achaemenid dynasty - where three

48

enormous royal tents and fifty-nine smaller ones, just so everyone knew their place, were painstakingly arranged in a star-shaped design. He told me how the best chefs from Maxim's of Paris had been flown in to prepare breast of peacock - the proud symbol of the Persian throne - for visiting dignitaries from around the world. The grand feast had apparently been served on Limoges china and the finest wines drunk from priceless Baccarat crystal. This blatant disparity between Iran's haves and have-nots led to a number of university students taking to the streets to protest at the injustice. But dissent and demonstrations were few and far between in Iran in the early 1970s, crushed with ferocious brutality by the Shah's henchmen. Still, the Shah of Iran was the self-styled guardian of the Persian Gulf, friend of the West and its interests, and recently back from an official visit to America where he was honoured as the distinguished guest of President Nixon and thus receiving the official seal of approval from the United States. For the moment at least, the Shah's position looked as enduring as the ancient Iranian monarchy itself.

Chapter 7: The Long Arm of the Shah

Both his Imperial Majesty and the Empress Farah were regular visitors to performances at Talar Roudaki. As a visit from his royal benefactors drew near, Mr. Ahmadzadeh would become increasingly agitated. He knew the stakes and who called the shots. Our stocky, plump-faced director would march into the studio, sweeping the coiffed black hair from his forehead. Although limited in his knowledge of classical ballet and rather lacking in artistic flair, he dismissed our experienced Russian dance master and took over rehearsals himself. The stress-induced dark rings under his eyes and thick black eyebrows collapsed into a deep frown, signalling to company members that the day's rehearsals were likely to be a protracted affair. Having hijacked the proceedings in this way, he wasted no time in pointing a stubby finger at an Iranian dancer - anyone would do - and boomed out: '*yek, doe, se, chehar* - one, two, three, four - *yek, doe, se, chehar*', his voice rising with each rhythmic count to four.

The day before royal visits no one was allowed into the theatre. All lockers in the changing rooms had to be cleared for rigorous security checks by the Imperial Guards. Our make-up boxes, *pointe* shoes, personal possessions and costumes had to be removed: anything left behind would be confiscated. On one occasion, I'd finished my rehearsal late and was swiftly escorted off the premises by a guard, bayonet in hand.

Performance night saw us taking extra care that our hair was well lacquered and tightly clipped into buns, shoe ribbons securely tied and heavy stage make-up meticulously applied. In the distance the sound of a helicopter engine above the theatre announced the arrival of the Imperial couple. With the national anthem *Sorood-e Shahanshahi Iran*, a suitably flattering chronicle of the various exploits of the Pahlavi dynasty duly completed, back stage tension was running high. Time for those pernickety final adjustments. Ballet-ribbons not too tight? Costumes well clasped, hair secure? The audience might well have been packed with dignitaries and specially invited guests, but as the rural first act of *Giselle*, one of the greatest of all the romantic classics, finally got underway, my mind was focused on only one couple - the Shah of Iran and his elegant wife the Shahbanou.

My role in *Giselle* was one of a pair of *wilis*. Needless to say this was an occasional source of mild amusement to one or two of the native English speakers in the company, though the rather juvenile double entrendre wore thin over time. The genre of *ballet blanc* - an ethereal setting with the female corps wearing long, white tulle skirts - originated with *Giselle*, the 19th-century's most symbolic of classical ballets. A hush fell over audience and orchestra alike, all eyes focused on the conductor and his silver baton. The corps de ballet waited in the wings as Adolphe Adam's enchanting music set about transforming the atmosphere inside Talar Roudaki. Then, with heightened concentration, an additional round of nerves and a burst of energy, we ran balletically onto the stage, gracing it with precision lines, confusing circles and startling still poses. With hours of rehearsals behind us, our movements became almost automatic, and all that remained was for us to immerse ourselves totally into *wilis*, the ghosts of maidens who had died before their wedding day. That did not mean that there was no time for humour. I remember being slightly distracted on one occasion as Ros whispered to me, deadly serious in tone, 'and always remember, Clair, that hell hath no fury like a *wili* scorned.'

It was during the interval of one performance of *Giselle* that Arash called me. I could tell that he had something important to to say, something in confidence, the prospect of which pleased me. I wondered if he was about to whisper that he too was finding it difficult to conceal his true feelings of affection. Fully-kitted in the dark green costume of Hilarian, the game-keeper desperately in love with *Giselle*, it turned out that romance was the last thing on his mind.

'You see that guy over there?' he said, pointing out an Iranian dancer by the name of Behrouz who was walking off-stage. Elfin-faced and slight of build, he was a competent performer in the company. I nodded. 'He's a spy', he said in disgust. 'What?' I retorted. 'Mr. Ahmadzadeh has spies in the company?' He chuckled at my innocence. I think he must have found my naïvety endearing, an innocent abroad, literally so, and therefore necessary to be taken under his wing. 'That's right - he works for Savak, the secret police.'

You didn't need to be an expert in the murky world of Iranian politics to know that Savak - the acronym for the *Sazeman-e Ettela'at va Amniyat-e Keshvar* or National Intelligence and Security Organisation - was no laughing matter. In South Africa I'd seen at close quarters how politics and the arts were inextricably bound together. So too now in Iran.

Given his anti-Shah views, I wondered if Arash might be in danger 'Of course I am,' he said quietly. 'Everyone is. Informants like Behrouz - they are two a penny in Iran and have infiltrated all walks of life.' He explained that they tracked individuals considered threats to the Shah's regime - poets, professors, filmmakers and students - no one was immune. Arash lit a cigarette and moved closer to me. He must have picked up my anguish. 'Don't worry about me, though - I know how to play the game. Just watch what you say and don't be fooled by his easy-going manner.'

I learned that the National Intelligence and Security Organisation had thousands of agents on the payroll. As many as one third of Iranian men were thought to have some kind of connection to Savak, either as active agents or as informants, like Behrouz. I was appalled at the notion of Savak operating within the ballet company, aware that its watchwords were murder and execution - torture it's tried and tested technique.

Chapter 8: A Hidden Identity

Returning to my flat after the brief walk back from Talar Roudaki, I heard the telephone ringing.   I rushed to pick up the receiver.   It was my cousin Martin Watts.   Unlike my mother, he had anglicised his name from Wartski.   We had met only once before when my family first moved to London.   My mother had mentioned that he might well try and track me down in Tehran.   He told me he was in Iran working as an archaeologist and was now managing a site a few hours' drive away.   Would Karen and I be interested in getting away for the weekend to join him in a remote village not far from the dig? He said that it would be an opportunity to experience Iranian life away from the teeming metropolis of Tehran and as an additional sweetener mentioned that there might also well be a colourful local surprise for us to boot.   We could hardly accept quickly enough.

Martin arrived in his noisy jeep to pick us up.   Remembering his rugged good looks and thick silver-coloured hair,   I could hardly believe my luck - family in Iran. It was wonderfully refreshing to see the drab landscape and flat grey roof tops of Tehran disappear into the distance as we headed due north towards the Caspian Sea.   By mid-afternoon we pulled up outside a modern house with many outbuildings on a large plot of dry, dusty land. A casually-dressed portly man appeared, greeting us with a big smile. Martin introduced him rather grandly as the Khan, explaining that it means a respected person, not least because he provided work for the villagers.

'My friends,' said the Khan, 'you must be thirsty after your drive. Come indoors where we shall relax and drink *chai*.' Large oriental mirrors with ornate gold frames adorned the walls and on the floors Persian carpets of intricate designs and bold colours were spread out. The long table in the centre of the dining room was covered with terrines overflowing with fresh and dried fruit while an ornate samovar spluttered in the background in preparation for the tea.   Everything was thoughtfully set out on stainless steel platters placed around the table. We sat in upright wooden chairs as female servants from the village made sure that our plates were never empty and our small tea glasses remained full.   With dining formalities completed, the Khan was keen to show us the outhouses where women and children worked on carpets with complex patterns and motifs, some of which were on display in his living room. Karen and I were invited to stay overnight.

Shortly after sunset we were ushered into a small room. It was as though we had been transported into the mystical world of one of the ballet company's exotic oriental productions, the dim lighting accentuating the decorative floor candles and sending staccato shadows darting in each and every direction. Close by was an elaborate hubbly-bubbly, its coiled snake-like hose giving off a most peculiar aroma. We were invited to relax on the large floor cushions, each of us taking turns to inhale the tobacco smoke. Before long my head began to spin. I made my excuses and stumbled off to bed.

'My friends', bellowed the jovial Khan the following morning, as we enjoyed warm *naan* bread with goat's cheese. 'I am happy you have come and tonight there is more entertainment for you.'

Karen and I had no difficulty in convincing one another that we could get away with missing one day of work and we decided to stay on. That evening the Khan laid on an outdoor show for his guests. He clapped his hands and two bearded men appeared carrying *dayereh*, Persian frame drums, followed by five female folk dancers dressed in traditional sequined costumes, their hair covered by long flowing scarves. The skilful handling of the metal pieces attached to the *dayereh* provided a tambourine-like quality which served to accentuate the dancers' sensual movements, flowing arms circling seductively above heads, their dark eyes remaining firmly fixed on the Khan throughout. Every movement choreographed to entice and excite, it was a wonderfully refreshing contrast to the world of classical ballet which by comparison suddenly seemed so stuffy and staid. The Khan sat surrounded by his guests, content with the display - pride written all over his well-fed face.

When we finally returned to Talar Roudaki it was time to face music of a different kind. It was immediately clear that Mr. Ahmadzadeh was not best pleased - we were both in trouble. 'Where have you been?' he demanded. 'We were about to get the police to come and find you had you not returned. Where have you been?' he repeated. 'This is no back street club you know. Let me remind you that we are the National Ballet Company of Iran, and we don't need girls like you damaging our reputation.'

'Today,' he continued 'you will not join in class. I may send the two of you back to London right away.' It soon emerged, however, that Mr. Ahmadzadeh's shocking threat was designed to shake us up rather than send us home, since he informed us the following day that we were to be granted a reprieve. No explanation was given and needless to say we did not insist upon one being provided. I suspected that he was anxious to avoid the consequences of two Royal Ballet school dancers being expelled and the complications that might have entailed in terms of future recruitment and auditions. Still, an arbitrary, fudged decision was fine by us and nothing was mentioned of our dastardly deeds ever again. Instantly forgiven, instantly forgotten. That was Iran.

In fact Mr. Ahmadzadeh's full forgiveness was forthcoming more speedily than I could have imagined. Karen and I were invited, along with every member of the company, to a lunch reception at his house the following Friday. His impressive one-storey residence was situated in the affluent northern suburbs of Tehran, home to Iran's bourgeoisie and hidden from prying eyes by a high security fence. Imposing wrought iron gates opened onto a well-kept garden with luxuriant green lawns.

Aida Ahmadzadeh greeted us with a warm smile, her dark hair carefully combed back, accentuating the hallmark heavy make-up around her dark, shining eyes. Amid the enticing smell of nutmeg and cinnamon, she handed me *havij bastani*, a carrot juice ice-cream float garnished with savoury spices. In the warm embrace of Iranian hospitality, I sampled a wide variety of traditional Persian cuisine - a refreshing yogurt and cucumber dip, baklava, halva, dried figs and *nargesi esfanaaj* - fried spinach with eggs and onions - the delicate collision of flavours a treat to the palate. As the dishes continued to flow thick and fast, it was a pleasant surprise to see that behind the grey tie and starched white shirt he wore for work, Mr. Ahmadzadeh could be light-hearted and fun as he went out of his way to ensure that everyone's needs, gastronomic or otherwise, were met with kindness and consideration.

The temperature was well into the 30s and most of the guests headed towards the oval-shaped pool. By now, of course, I knew all company members by name but this was the first opportunity for everyone to spend time together at a purely social occasion. At work most of the communication was in English, but here the Iranians tended to speak in Farsi. I tried in vain to pick up a word or two, short phrases I might get the gist of. Arash spoke the best English of all the Iranians in the company, and I couldn't help but notice how at ease he was in the company of the English-speaking girls. I was about to check if that observation had been a little hasty when I saw him whisked away to bask in the flattery of the darker-skinned Persian women too. I saw that Arash was equally at ease in the company of these Iranian beauties and, more worryingly for me, that the opposite was also true, as they giggled and fussed around him. These envious thoughts were brought to an abrupt halt when Mr. Ahmadzadeh called us to lunch. It was difficult to believe that the impressive array of dishes already served were just by way of *hors d'œuvres*.

Two round tables laden with exotic culinary fare were placed side by side. Enormous platters of steaming rice with a powdering of saffron were placed alongside succulent barbecued chicken, lamb, spicy grilled tomatoes and *dolme barg*, vine leaves wrapped around ground meat and herbs. Mr. Ahmadazdeh insisted that I sample Iranian ice-cream. Rich and sweet thanks to its generous toppings of finely-chopped pistachio nuts and honey, I discovered not only why this was one of his favourite desserts but also how he come to acquire such an ample waistline.

I appreciated the sense of belonging I experienced at the Ahmadzadehs, but it also underlined my isolation from my own family and culture. It suddenly occurred to me that in Tehran I did have an extended family, of sorts, the thriving Jewish community in Persia, one of the oldest of the Diaspora, with roots reaching back to Biblical times. I wondered whether or not the time was now right to make contact. My parents had repeatedly suggested that I should do so but consistent with the greater part of their advice given at that time, I had steadfastly ignored it.

Although the Jews of Iran had been through good times and bad during almost 3,000 years of history, no one disputed that the reign of the Shah was their golden era. They accounted for only a tiny percentage of Iran's population - albeit the largest Jewish population of any Muslim country in the world - yet the Jews of Persia were extremely well represented among Iran's business community, holding key positions in the oil industry, banking and law, as well as in Tehran's traditional bazaar. Two of the eighteen members of the Iranian Academy of Sciences were Jews, as were 600 of the country's 10,000 physicians. There was one additional statistic that struck a chord - that to the best of my knowledge the Iranian National Ballet Company had just one Jewish employee on its payroll - me.

Not that I was a practising or religious Jew. I hardly paid any attention to the Jewish religious festivals, didn't keep a kosher home - in fact if truth be told you could always count me in for an egg and bacon fry-up. Nor would you be likely to find a *mezuzah*, a piece of parchment contained in a decorative case and inscribed with ancient Hebrew verses, affixed to any doorframe in my home, rented or otherwise. My family used to observe the High Holy days during my childhood in South Africa and my brother had celebrated his *Bar mitzvah* at a traditional synagogue in the Johannesburg suburb of Berea. We were what some people rather condescendingly referred to as 'chopped liver' Jews - fond of Ashkenazi cuisine, warmly embracing our rich cultural heritage - but certainly not in the premier league when it came to matters spiritual.

So I was hardly likely to dash to the sabbath services taking place in my newly adopted host city. Which was a shame, in many respects, because had I done so I would have discovered the ancient Yusufabad Synagogue of Tehran, regularly packed to capacity with men in skull caps and tallit shawls, rhythmically reading from the Torah, their words little changed since the days of the Old Testament.

I harboured not the slightest hesitation when it came to telling Arash that I was Jewish. I certainly had no intention of keeping it a secret. Why should I? After all, he was a progressive Muslim and I a liberal Jew. 'Oh', he said, slightly taken aback, but covering it well with a half-smile. In fact a protracted theological debate was positively the

59

last thing on our minds. We had far more of an appetite for stories relating to each other's families and friends, lapping up new names and places, any snippet of information, no matter how trivial, enthusiastically embraced. As we did so, we failed to notice the days and weeks go by. We shared intimate thoughts and feelings and contrasted our different lives which, not so very long ago, had been so far apart but now, by a strange twist of fate, were becoming increasingly intertwined. We were, superficially at least, an unlikely couple - a Jewish South African and an Iranian Muslim, together in the Middle East where the values of the Koran, for the devout and non-believers alike, impacted on all aspects of social, political and economic life. I would listen as Arash described Persian notions of hospitality and charity, politics and poverty, education and morality. He seemed so kind and compassionate in his analyses. Entranced by his eloquent words and eager to learn more of his vision for a fair and prosperous Iran, it seemed that our friendship had taken on a momentum of its own. We had become inseparable. Laughing, teasing one another, dancing and dining together, my mind was awash with novel notions, my body overwhelmed with equally new sensations of excitement and arousal. As I soaked in these fresh and fascinating perspectives on life in Iran, there was one fact of which I was already entirely certain - that I never wanted to be parted from Arash.

Still, his take on Jewish history and its implications for the politics of the Middle East would surface from time to time. They were not easy moments between us. 'I am not denying that the Holocaust actually happened', Arash said somewhat nonchalantly one day, while driving his khaki coloured Mini Moke en route to Talar Roudaki, 'but I do question the numbers.' I was staggered and bewildered, staring at him in disbelief. 'Well, six million Jews murdered could very well be an exaggeration.' Up until that moment I had only the greatest respect for his judgement - but now he might as well have slapped me in the face. I was so shocked at his remarks that it took me a few moments to gather my thoughts. 'You simply can't say that, Arash. The facts and figures relating to the holocaust have been well documented by historians. And I can tell you something else - that amongst the many millions who perished in the concentration camps were members of my own family - members of the Wartski family who were stuck in Poland and who couldn't get out in time.'

'I'm sorry, Clair, I know that there were terrible atrocities committed. I am not denying that. All I am saying is that you can't trust everything you read. Six million Jews murdered could very well be an exageration.' Just as I had grown to admire his wealth of knowledge and generosity of spirit during the last few months, so now his words, with their revisionist and anti-Semitic undertone, left me feeling distinctly raw and shakey. I might well have been only an occasional visitor to the synagogues of Johannesburg and London but now I felt the need to defend what I perceived to be an unjustified assault on my birthright and heritage. And yet at the same time I felt sure that Arash would not deliberately mislead me. Whatever the case, for the very first time I felt uneasy in his presence. Certainly he had opened my eyes to what was really going on in Iran. Yet I shuddered as he continued with his broad and sweeping assertions. 'Maybe it is the case that the Holocaust - whatever the truth about the numbers - is being used for political purposes or to elicit support for Israel - that cancer in the Middle East' I was ashamed of myself for lacking the historical knowledge to counter his narrative. As a naïve, 20-year-old dancer who had left high school without a single educational certificate to my name, I felt ill-equipped to engage in political debate - let alone launch into a staunch defence of the complex issues relating to the legitimacy of the Jewish state.

Maybe it was for these reasons - in truth I am not entirely sure. But in the event I decided that I would be better off keeping my distance from Iran's ancient Jewish community. In doing so I turned my back on the dozens of synagogues in Tehran and gave a wide berth to the Kaurosh Kabir Hospital, perhaps the most venerable institution of Iranian Jewry famed for providing free or heavily subsidised health care to the poor and needy in Tehran. In general terms I simply closed my eyes to the many very visible signs of Jewish life in the city centre - which happened to include various youth movements, numerous shops supplying kosher provisions, Jewish women's institutions, a Jewish Students' Union, Jewish charities, a Jewish nursery, a Jewish Graduates' Association and an Iranian Jewish Committee known as *Anjoman-e Kalimian-e Iran*. I felt uncomfortable with this part of my identity.   Best then to keep it under wraps.   I tried to convince myself that I wouldn't be missing out on that much in any event - it was not as if the time-honoured traditions of Judaism were flowing through my veins.   It was a strategy which proved only partially successful as my sense of unease would continue to linger for some time.

Chapter 9: Homeward Bound?

The Iranian National Ballet was flourishing. This was in no small part thanks to Inga and Robert Urazgildief, the young Russian couple brought over from the Kirov Ballet to assist the Iranian National Ballet in continuing to raise its game. Mr. Ahmadzadeh might not have been an artist himself but he certainly knew where to find talent, in this instance at the former Imperial Russian Ballet in Leningrad, one of the world's leading classical companies. Madame Inga's and Monsieur Robert's superb classes were an art form in themselves, enhancing the dancers' technical skills and inspiring artistic flair. Iran might well have been a trusted political ally of the West but the Shah was canny enough to have spread his wings far and wide, creating a series of cultural exchanges with the Soviet Union, ensuring that we were amongst those fortunate enough to regularly train and perform with the very best dancers from the Eastern bloc. My particular style of ballet, dismissed so disparagingly by the Royal Ballet School's formidable Miss Fewster - 'too Russian' was the phrase still ringing in my ears - was at long last coming into its own.

It was a similar story with Tilde Urseanu, a Romanian choreographer brought to Tehran to stage *Bolero*, Ravel's orchestral marvel and most well-known composition. With its distinctive, steady rhythm and repetitive theme, the rehearsals for *Bolero* were engaging and exciting as the production quickly began to take shape. The tempo began gently enough, the lighting dim and mysterious as dancers appeared line by line like shadows from the back of a slightly raised but entirely bare stage. Women wore eye-catching yellow and black swishing skirts attached to tight bodices revealing just a hint of cleavage, whilst the men were magnificent as *toreadors* in well fitting smart black suits. My dark hair was tightly bound in a large bun, eye make-up used to maximum effect. Whether or not fate lent a helping hand I don't know, but I was only too delighted to perform the role of a spirited Spanish *senorita* to my designated partner - Arash. The pace quickened as the sensual tension, so evident in the music, metamorphosed into movement. The rich and haunting variety of timbres raced through our souls, limbs and bodies intertwining to the rising crescendo of the famously percussive score.

As the weeks went by Arash and I could hardly bear to be apart, enjoying quiet moments picnicking together, walking through *Jamshidieh*, one of the most picturesque parks in Tehran, or leaving the capital city for weekend outings to the Caspian, which Arash explained was classed by some as the world's largest lake, by others as a fully-fledged sea. When alone I would imagine his eyes focusing on my face, as we danced to the driving beat of *Bolero*, its intense melody coaxing and enticing us on.

Late one Thursday afternoon after a long day's rehearsals, Arash accompanied me back to my flat. 'Stay for a snack', I suggested. 'Karen won't be back till late and I've enough Bolognese to feed an army.'   Supper out of the way, it seemed immodest to speak the unspeakable, to say out loud what we were both undoubtedly longing for. So instead we dodged the awkward silence, threw some cushions down on the carpet and snuggled up close together on the lounge floor. Inevitably in the quiet of the warm room, the uncomfortable barriers soon melted away as we became lost in the heat and intimacy of tender love-making, a meeting of minds and bodies that had gone far beyond even the suggestive, pulsating beat of *Bolero*.   Finally, exhausted and in silence, we lay in each other's embrace, quite still, watching the dusk turn to night.

And then, quite bizarrely, Arash disappeared. Phone messages went unanswered. Everyone at work was anxious for news but no one more so than me.   Maybe I had misjudged Arash, maybe falling into his arms and making love had been a mistake and now I would have to pay the price. At home I waited for his now familiar knock at the door. But it was not forthcoming. In my desperation I even imagined him standing outside on the step, looking up towards our flat, picturing his cheeky smile and intense brown eyes.   Of course all of that changed nothing - the reality was that there was no sign of him at all. I wondered what I might have done to upset him.   I went through it in my mind time and again. All I could recall from our last encounter was a whirl of intimacy and excitement - explosive sensations which I had not experienced before.   Surely he could not be harbouring misgivings about that.

We had just turned into our road on our way home from Talar Roudaki when Karen grabbed my arm. 'Clair', she said discreetly, 'he's there'. I froze, my heart thumping as though it would burst through my chest. 'I'll go off and visit Ros and leave you two alone'. Then, looking at me, she added a little apprehensively, 'unless you want me to stay, that is?' 'No Karen, thanks, I think I have got to deal with this alone. I'll be fine.' As I continued towards the front door I could see Arash looking at me - no, staring at me - and I immediately noticed his pale face, dishevelled hair and the dark rings under his eyes. A sense of foreboding began to cloud my thoughts.

As we climbed the stairs up to the apartment, I was angry with Arash. What on earth had come over him? Try as I might, I found it impossible to conceal the hurt in my voice when, finally, I blurted out the blindingly obvious question: where had he been? Ignoring the legitimacy of my enquiry, he turned to me and said, 'you were not a virgin'. I could feel the pain in each of his words, unexpected and unfair though they be. 'Er, n-no', I stammered, bemused by his pronouncement. 'Well', he continued slowly, 'this has come as a great shock to me, Clair. I haven't been able to sleep or eat. I couldn't face anyone at work, especially you. In fact, if you want to know the truth I have actually been feeling physically sick.'

To say that I was shocked at his outburst would be something of an understatement. I had never pretended to be something that I was not. Indeed, the entire issue of my virginity, or its absence, to be more precise, had never really crossed my mind. But the onslaught had still to run its course. 'It was just that I somehow expected you to be different, more innocent, unlike so many Western girls who come out to Iran.' So that was it. I had been the cause of his malaise. Still, it was all beyond me, somehow quite absurd. 'Arash, do I have a sexual past?', I asked rhetorically. 'Of course I do.' I was 20 years old, after all, and whilst not exactly a free-spirited child of the swinging sixties I had still spent two years as a student in London. I plucked up the courage to continue. 'And I dare say that you have had more than a few adventures yourself.' He was clearly troubled and I felt a shiver run through my body as I waited for his response. But his large tired eyes simply blanked me out as he turned away, already deep in his own thoughts.

If this was going to be the breaking point of our fledgling relationship, then I could certainly do nothing about it. I steadied myself and tried to gather my thoughts during the uncomfortable moments of silence. Was there any form of words which might help my point of view come across more easily? Any tone of phrase which might help soften the blow? If there were, they escaped me. It only remained for him to turn around and walk out of the flat and out of my life. But he did not. Instead, slowly, he turned towards me. I could see the tears he had been fighting back. His face seemed sad but more reconciled, more forgiving. In silence he gestured me towards him and we stayed motionless holding tightly onto one another for what seemed an inordinate amount of time.

Although I was taken aback by Arash's outburst - it wasn't the first sign of erratic behaviour I'd witnessed - nor would it be the last. I hadn't made a fuss the first time he turned up over an hour late, his kiss smelling of alcohol. The truth was I had fallen deeply in love and could forgive him anything and everything. It seemed as if my emotions were an unstoppable force with a momentum of their own. He was my Persian prince and I loved him.

Ten months after my arrival in Tehran the time had come to return home. My contract had been renewed by mutual agreement for a second year, entitling me to one month's summer holiday. I was barely more than my parents' little girl when I set off for Tehran, and as a child I'd always been reluctant to leave the security of home. How all that had changed. I had found the man, a complex person, admittedly - but a wonderful human being with whom I had every intention of sharing my life. He too clearly had issues of his own to deal with, not least in relation to my past which evidently weighed heavily on his mind. But in the event that had not prevented him from taking me into his heart. We were in love. It was unthinkable to contemplate anything other than of our futures being permanently intertwined.

As the wheels of the Iran Air jumbo jet touched down on the runway at London's Heathrow airport, I wondered how I was going to break my big news.

Flinging our arms around one another in a tight embrace, it was kisses all round. 'Thank God you're home, Clair. I'm never going to let you go again.' My father's emotional reserve slipped and I knew these words came straight from his heart. Which of course made it all the more difficult for me to reply. 'Daddy,' I said, 'I've fallen in love and I want to go back to Iran and marry Arash.'

Chapter 10: A Tale of Two Fathers

He had spent the best part of his career in the service of the Imperial Armed Forces of Iran - the Shah's army. Always immaculately turned out in a double breasted suit, standing tall and proud, his well-tended moustache a case-study in the mathematics of symmetry, Parviz Alizadeh had worked his way steadily up through the military hierarchy, rising to the rank of Colonel. He had demonstrated an equally determined and disciplined approach in his relentless, and ultimately successful, pursuit of Shahin, an elegant Turkish woman who had become the mother of their five children - Arash the eldest at 24, Shahla, Shideh and Sholeh, her three daughters aged 22, 17 and 15 respectively and a mischievous 8 year old son by the name of Babak. Situated in the smart middle-class suburbs of northern Tehran, the Alizadehs lived in a neighbourhood known as Gholhak where, years earlier, the British had built an extensive complex which served as an ambassadorial residence. Its ownership had been granted to the British government by Mohammad Shah Qajar, the Shah of Persia during the Qajar dynasty, relations then so cordial and colonial that the rural people of the area were considered British subjects, exempt from Iranian rule. The Alizadeh family's residence might not have been so grand - their house was a spacious 3-storey home in leafy Banafsheh Street - but that did not prevent a constant stream of family and friends from stopping by for a chat over a glass of *chai* or Turkish coffee - sometimes served up with sweet biscuits and fruit but always accompanied by a truly warm welcome, the hallmark of Iranian hospitality. Given this backdrop of stability and success, one might be excused for thinking that Parviz Alizadeh would have worn the look of a contented man on his face. But he did not. For the very simple reason that he had never really considered ballet dancing as a possible career option on the slowly-constructed but very thorough list of dreams and aspirations which, over the years, he had painstakingly established for his eldest son.

Inevitably these frustrations with his first born would spill over from time to time - with stern words being spoken. Why was it that Arash steadfastly refused to complete his architectural studies? Was he unwilling or unable - or both? Was it not shameful, and a matter of some dishonour to his family, that he categorically refused to be conscripted into the army? Why was it not possible for him to go out and find himself a proper job? 'And what kind of job should that be?' Arash would enquire. 'I don't know exactly', Parviz would retort, his tone of disappointment not difficult to detect, 'but the further away from the world of ballet and Talar Roudaki, then the better it would be.'

In her role as peace-maker Shahin knew that she had her work cut out. Constantly trying to smooth ruffled feathers, a look of reluctant resignation could often be seen in her kind brown eyes, her life dedicated to the large family which she cared for with an unflagging generosity of spirit. With round-the-clock help from Mansoureh, a young peasant girl who had become the family's live-in help, every morning she would buy fresh vegetables and an assortment of green herbs known as *sabzi* before embarking on the long and elaborate preparations relating to the day's meals. Hours would be spent sitting at the large round kitchen table, where she would carefully sift through every grain of rice checking for small stones before washing the ample quantities three times in preparation. Shahin had patiently taught Mansoureh everything she knew - literacy included - since her arrival as a young girl of thirteen from a remote village some ten years earlier. Her head covered by a scarf, even when indoors, Mansoureh had proved herself a keen student. '*Chanum, chanum*' she would shout out to Shahin, '*Madam, madam*, listen to me read'.

Shahin was so kindly and caring, in fact, that her warm-heartedness extended to those animals fortunate enough to come within her care. So it was that, in the bitterly cold winter nights of Tehran, she would bring in the few lambs that had been out in the garden, provide them with shelter in a disused room at the bottom of the house, supply ample offerings of food and water before letting them out again into the following morning's early crisp sunshine. With a helping hand from Mansoureh she would then embark upon the unenviable task of scrubbing down and sterilising the room so thoroughly that within an hour or so no one could ever have imagined that it had doubled up as a temporary animal sanctuary. Her children all doted on her as she helped them with their homework or needlework - Shahin holding the Alizadeh family together with a blend of tolerance and patience but above all an apparently unlimited amount of love.

I had seen this for myself when Arash decided to introduce me to his family. Shortly prior to the end of my first year's contract with the ballet company I had been invited to his home. It was clearly a significant step for us both. Sensing my nerves as we drove towards the northern suburbs of Tehran, he raised his voice slightly so as to be heard above the noise coming from the engine of his Mini Moke. 'Don't worry Clair, all my family are really looking forward to meeting you'. Taking his eyes off the road for a split second he glanced at me, adding 'there are a lot of us, but I am sure that you'll get the hang of it in no time'. I remained worried about the language barrier, my Farsi having hardly come along at all. 'Clair', he said, reassuringly, 'apart from my parents and younger brother, all my sisters speak English, so there's really no problem.' Arash was right - my initial nerves disappeared almost immediately upon arrival at Banafsheh Street. Arash's father, Parviz, kept himself slightly at arm's length, true enough, but other than that everyone seemed to share Arash's kindly manner and natural warmth. 'Clair, would you like a cup of Turkish coffee?', Sholeh, the youngest of the three daughters asked. Young Babak, intrigued at the sight of an unusual guest in his home smiled at me, his happy spirit shining through his large soulful brown eyes. Desperate to communicate, he rattled off a sentence or two in rapid fire Farsi. 'Babak *jaan*,' interrupted Sholeh kindly, 'Clair doesn't understand you - so you see how important it is for you to work hard in your English lessons. Turning her attention to me, she added, 'he is trying to tell you, Clair, that I make the best Turkish coffee in the house'. Holding onto his small hands I replied, 'well in that case I would love a cup'. He glanced up towards his sister, anxious to know my answer, proud that I had given him all of my attention.

I was especially anxious to communicate with Arash's mother, Shahin, but apart from a few basic words, the ancient Persian language had been far too difficult for me to master. With the patient help of all my new found interpreters though Shahin and I were able to interact effectively. Sufficiently so, at any rate, for me to understand that she was welcoming me most warmly into the heart of the Alizadeh family. As the evening wore on, she suggested to Arash that I stay the night. 'You can sleep in my room Clair', Shideh, the middle sister, suggested. 'And I'll share with Sholeh *jaan*'. In no time at all,

71

everything had been sorted. I was delighted to have the opportunity of staying over and rather shyly I came out with one of my few phrases - *khei'li mot-sha'keram*. It was not exactly a master-class in modern linguistics - it only meant 'thank you very much' but I could see that the astute and generous-hearted Shahin was reading me loud and clear.

I had managed to convince my parents to travel to Tehran and meet Arash and his family. Instead of trying to dissuade me from pursuing my romance, they had rapidly come to the conclusion that the most prudent course of action was to come out to Iran for a fortnight with a view to seeing the lay of the land. Perhaps they had sensed that they were up against an unstoppable force. In any event, they said that they were anxious to see Roudaki Hall and, better still, me performing in one of the great classical ballets. Whatever the case, I could hardly believe my luck - the people I loved most were now poised to meet up and I was full of confidence for the best of all possible outcomes. They were bound to adore Arash, just as I did. After all, he had such impeccable manners, spoke very fluent English - albeit with just a tiny hint of a Persian accent - which, to my eyes, made him all the more irresistible. And he was, by any standards, very handsome indeed. I convinced myself that only the briefest interlude would be required before they too would come to see him through my eyes. Not for the first time, here was a judgement about which I was to be proved wrong.

Not that I harboured even the slightest doubt that the Alizadehs would do anything other than provide a warm welcome, for warm welcomes were their natural stock-in-trade. With a helping hand from Mansoureh, Shahin had seen to it that everything was ready and in place to ensure that my parents, Sheila and Duke, would feel at home in Iran. Now it was their turn to be ushered into the spacious lounge overlooking the garden and small swimming pool towards the back of the house, Arash stepping forward to introduce himself, my heart bursting with pride. The warm smiles of Shahin and Parviz were immediately reassuring. Babak gave a shy grin, lighting up his intelligent face and accentuating large brown eyes shaded by long dark eyelashes. Darting in and out of the lounge, he was happy to lend a helping hand, bringing in generous platters of fresh and dried fruit, a vast selection of different nuts, sweet biscuits and tea. Still unused to the presence of foreign guests in his home, he snuggled up to his mother who looked at him reassuringly.   When, a little later, the three sisters entered an appearance their fluent English helped to overcome the atmosphere of awkwardness that had lingered in the lounge, despite earlier efforts of small talk relating to flights out from London and the delights of hotel accommodation in Tehran.

In a determined attempt to communicate more effectively my mother endeavoured to slow down the natural rhythm of her speech, articulating every syllable more clearly and, in an impromptu attempt to ensure that there could be little risk of her message not coming across, with large and dramatic arm movements, as if performing on stage.   An unconventional approach, undoubtedly, but her natural theatricality seemed to be doing the trick, as the two mothers appeared not just to be understanding one another rather easily but bonding in the process too, the absence of a common language evidently no impediment to effective communication or the creation of friendship and goodwill.   This was in stark contrast to the conduct of the two fathers - Parviz and Duke - who retained their natural reserve, giving little to nothing away of their true thoughts relating to the rather strained proceedings unfolding before them.   Whilst my mother remained upbeat and effusive throughout, my father was introspective and pensive - signs that were familiar to me and that did not augur well.   Still, it was an extraordinary meeting of people from different cultures, countries and faiths.   But as the gathering drew to a close, I was desperate to find out what his private reflections were about.   All I was seeking was his seal of approval.   Was that really such a lot to ask?

The following day Arash and I set off, together with my parents, to visit the chaotic and noisy grand bazaar of Tehran, in the run-down southern section of the city.   Here was the pulsating heart of the Iranian capital - known locally as 'the city within the city' because its ten kilometres of corridors packed with shops and stalls represented an economic powerhouse making it the largest market of its kind anywhere in the world. Among its labyrinth of winding alleyways we had the impression that it was possible to find just about anything the human mind had ever conceived - from exquisite priceless hand woven silk carpets to broken television sets and electrical items - with just about everything else available for purchase in between. This included copper, paper, spices, precious metals of all kinds, food, clothes, shoes, tools, leather goods, machines, books, stationery, perfumes, local artefacts, souvenirs and a vast range of pictures and portraits of Mohammad-Rezā Shāh Pahlavi, the Shah of Iran, available framed or unframed and in just about every size and shape imaginable. The grand bazaar also fulfilled a number of other functions than merely trade, playing host to banks, financiers, mosques and guest houses - with even a fire station sensibly thrown in for good measure.

They must have seen us coming. Because we were all too easily enticed with a 'hello, hello ... just look no buy. Come in I give you a cup of *chai*. Come and sit down, let us talk.' And before you could say 'Aladdin's cave' we would be sipping tea served from a samovar through a cube of sugar, and haggling over the prices of a series of small Persian rugs that we didn't really want or need.

No doubt it did not constitute the best timing on Arash's part. But when it came to politics it was as if he could not hold himself back. And so it was that, in the middle of the surrounding chaos and confusion, my prospective husband tried to explain to my parents that the highly-conservative traders, or *bazaaris*, had come to feel very threatened by the Shah's headlong rush towards western-style industrialisation and were angry that they had yet to benefit from the vast sums of oil money in the country. They were concerned that they would come to be left behind economically with their status in society being reduced as a result. Arash explained that although he did not share the conservative politics of the *bazaaris*, he was certainly able to identify with their disapproval of the Shah's regime. Not that my parents were overly attentive. They had other worries on their minds.

Chapter 11: A Passport to Matrimony?

After the energy and excitement of the hot and sticky bazaar, I was more than happy to beat a hasty retreat to my parents' hotel room on Pahlavi Street. I could easily forgive its drabness on the grounds that it boasted new and effective air-conditioning. Lined with shops, restaurants and kiosks, Pahlavi Street had been built by order of the Reza Shah Pahlavi, father of the ruling Shah and, unsurprisingly perhaps, had immediately acquired the name of their dynasty. At a little under 20 kilometres, it was the longest stretch of road in the Middle East, one of dozens of firsts which the Shah had been busily notching up for his regime. Arash had returned to the family home in Banafsheh Street, leaving me to share a private moment with my parents. I was happy to be with them - just the three of us. But I could feel an underlying tension, uncomfortable silences broken only by occasional mutterings from my father who was plainly mulling things over in his mind. As he looked over at me his eyes were heavy, his demeanour contemplative and sad.

'What is it? What is it daddy?'

'Clair,' he said, knowing that what he was about to say related to his duty as a father but regretting it all the same.

'Yes dad, what is it?' I glanced at my mother who sat at a small table on which various tourist leaflets about Tehran were set out, but her eyes remained firmly fixed on her husband.

'Darling, I know what I'm going to say is not going to please you. But it has to be said. I don't have to tell you how much I love you, and that what I say comes from a genuine desire to see you happy. But in my opinion, and I think your mother is with me on this, a union with Arash is fraught with problems right from the very off.'

I stared deeply into his eyes - daring to hope for a brief moment that this was some sort of a silly joke, a prank on his part and that at any second I would see his lips part and break into a broad smile whereupon we would all burst out and laugh together. But there were no signs of that. Could it be that he did not like or approve of

Arash? Was he unable to see an intelligent, kind and sensitive man, so selfless and attentive to the needs of others?

'Mum and I have been talking for much of the night, and we are not at all convinced that Arash is right for you.' I was stunned by my father's reflections. 'I can see how much you love Arash - of that there can be no doubt - and I'm sure he loves you too. But it would be less than honest of me if I simply sat back and said nothing. I just couldn't do that. So I must tell you that I am not at all happy with his situation.'

'Dad,' I said trying to keep my voice calm, 'he is studying for his final architectural diploma and he works part time for the ballet company.' I could hear not only my own irregular breathing, but ill-constructed excuses spilling from my mouth, apparently to little or no effect.

'I understand', retorted my father, 'Arash has been explaining all to me. We had a chat yesterday, and he was certainly very open and honest.' Then came the body blow. 'Of course our biggest worry is that Arash', he cleared his throat before proceeding, '... is that Arash, as you well know, doesn't have a passport'. I had been waiting for this to surface. 'And', he said pausing to look straight at me, 'unlikely to have one until he has completed his military service which, by my calculations, is likely to remain a good three years away. This would of course mean that you'll only ever be able to remain together whilst in Iran.' I was losing the argument.

'Daddy, I know it isn't a perfect situation, but honestly I couldn't bear to be without Arash. We are so suited - we laugh so much together. I didn't believe I could ever love someone so much and I simply can't let it go'.

My mother then intervened. 'I suggest this. Clair, you come back to London with us now. Give Arash a chance to finish his degree - it shouldn't take very long, he's only got to study for his final diploma. Then, after he has completed his military service, he can come over to London. In the meantime, you try to find yourself work in a London ballet company and wait for him there. How does that sound?'

'Oh no, no, no,' I heard myself say. 'That's a terrible idea.   That doesn't sound good at all. I can't leave Tehran and Arash'. I could feel the sadness in my heart just at the thought of being without him.

'Well', said my father, anxious that I shouldn't get so upset, 'tomorrow, we'll pay a visit to the British Embassy. They must have encountered similar situations before, and hopefully there will be somebody there to provide us with guidance on this whole issue of passports and we shall see if together we can't find a way through this.'

Set in a compound behind three metre walls on Ferdowsi Avenue in central Tehran, an embassy official was unable to provide the kind of reassurance for which I had been hoping. In fact the junior diplomat's message could hardly have been more clear-cut. Any British subject marrying an Iranian national immediately becomes an Iranian national too. From my point of view things were going from bad to worse and when I dared to glance towards my father I could see his face going ashen and grey. 'And what happens to her British passport?', he enquired. My passport, my passport, all my father could think about was my passport. It was so infuriating, he seemed to have become fixated on it. I wanted to scream out 'stop making such a fuss - please just trust my decision about Arash. He is so special, so utterly unique, the last thing he would ever do would be to inhibit my freedom. For goodness sake, he is desperate to find freedom for himself.' Had I said all of that aloud? Apparently not. I breathed a heavy sigh hoping to hear some good news.

'Well, she can keep it, of course', the embassay official replied. 'But unfortunately there would be no protection whatsoever that we here at the Embassy might be able to provide.   I repeat - she would henceforth be considered an Iranian subject and therefore accountable to the Iranian authorities and Iranian law.'

I could feel my head spinning as my father continued.

'And what exactly is the law for an Iranian woman who might wish to leave the country?' His voice was clear and precise.

'Oh', the official replied, 'a letter from her husband giving her written permission usually does the trick.' And with those words I knew my chances of convincing my father to allow me to marry in Iran had taken another battering. But it was only upon returning to my parents' hotel room that I came to realise just how far-reaching the fall-out from that meeting was likely to be.

This time, my father's voice was unapologetic and determined. 'We've found out important facts and met the lovely Alizadeh family. We've also had a fascinating visit to Iran. But Clair...' - I held my breath and waited for him to continue. 'As things stand, I really cannot give you my blessing to marry Arash. He has no passport and you would be in danger of losing your's. In fact, with no proper job, no home of his own, with two years of compulsory military service still to be completed, I really don't see Arash having a very clear vision of your future together at all. And without the very generous offer of living with his family after any marriage ceremony, you would be out on the streets. No thank you.' He repeated that phrase for good measure. 'No thank you. Not for my daughter. So as I see it Clair, you must go pack your bags, and return with us to London. I'm really very sorry darling, but that's it.'

It was then that I noticed a slightly salty taste in my mouth. As the tears trickled down my cheeks, I was quite unable to control a sobbing sound almost hiccupping out of my mouth. My mother put her arms around me but I felt a strange numbness. I was unwilling to be consoled. This was so far removed from the happy outcome that I had envisaged. During the course of the following days, I could feel a permanent tug of war taking place within my mind, Arash on the one side, my parents on the other. But for me there could be no doubt as to the ultimate outcome. There was simply no choice. For the first time in my life - not before time, perhaps - I could sense myself pulling away from my parents, from their counsel and protection. I had not the slightest intention of jumping on the first plane back to London and walking away from the man I loved.

Not insensitive to the problems of his would-be bride, Arash made a conscious effort to move matters forward himself. He was delighted to inform my parents that he had found a job in a firm of architects in which a first cousin, Karim, was employed. This unexpected news provided a timely boost to our battered spirits. It was not exactly a panacea to the myriad of problems which faced us, but it was at least something positive to bring to the table. It demonstrated that Arash would indeed one day be able to earn his keep as a fully qualified architect - meanwhile his cousin would sign off any drawings and designs for him. I hoped that my parents would be suitably impressed. But within 48 hours, he came back to me with more news - bad news. 'I handed in my notice Clair'. Stunned, I put my hands to my face. 'I'm sorry, but I had to, I had no choice.'

'I don't understand Arash, did they kick you out?'

'No, not at all, they rather liked me and tried to persuade me to stay.'

I could feel the disappointment knotting my stomach. 'So what happened?' I asked hesitantly, anticipating the problems this would inevitably cause.

'Clair, it was simple. It didn't take me long to realise that what I was being asked to design was part of a prison block for use by Savak - you know, the secret police.'

'Oh no,' I exhaled in frustration. I knew very well that Arash would never compromise his principles by having anything to do with the construction of such a building. In fact, if truth be told, I admired his readiness to take a stand against injustice and oppression. But what bad luck. What bad timing. How would I explain this to my parents? They would never understand his motives or the complex politics of Iran. It was difficult enough, after all, for his own father to comprehend.

Of course my father was distinctly unimpressed with what appeared to him to be a wholly cavalier approach to work and employment. 'Forty eight hours indeed', he scoffed. But weighing more heavily on his mind was the issue of my passport.

He looked tired and drawn but determined and alert at the same time. Despite the strain of the last few days his demeanour appeared to indicate that he might be receptive to innovative solutions, anything that could break us out of the current impasse. Clearing his throat, he attempted to sum up the situation. 'It seems to me to boil down to this. If you marry Arash, you will lose your British passport and all the rights that go with it. I cannot, I will not, allow that to happen. Never. But Clair, I can see your eyes sparkling with love every time you look at Arash.' I was unused to my father speaking so openly and emotionally. 'You are precious to us Clair, and we love you precisely because of these qualities.' My mother was looking down, but I could see her dabbing tears away from her cheeks with a small paper tissue. 'We don't want to lose you. We would never allow that to happen.' He continued. 'So how about this for a compromise?'

'I will give you my blessing to marry Arash, if....' - slowly and deliberately he repeated the word - 'if you can find a way of keeping your British passport.'

'Thank you, thank you so much.' I jumped onto my father's lap and gave him an enormous cuddle, just as I used to do when a young child. I had never imagined that I would hear those words coming from my father's lips. Although he was now smiling - as was my mother - it was clear to see that they had been spoken with a very heavy heart indeed. But they had been spoken just the same.

Chapter 12: A Most Unusual Wedding

The following day I was unexpectedly summonsed to appear before an *ad hoc* tribunal. One over which Arash had given himself jurisdiction and likewise appointed himself to preside. 'So how many were there then?' The tenderness had gone. Sitting himself down opposite me in the lounge, Arash's demeanor was serious as he firmly closed the double doors. Unable to decipher the reasons behind his latest malaise, I sat looking at him as a naughty schoolgirl would her teacher. What had I done wrong now? I immediately felt guilty as charged, although entirely unaware of any accusations against me. Not that I had to wait long to find out.

'It is absolutely vital, Clair', he began, 'that if we are to marry that I should know about your past boyfriends. All of them'.

So that was it. I breathed a sigh of relief, allowing myself a mischievous half-smile, knowing that not too much time would be required - it was not as if there was a long list to rattle through. But he retained his unblinking gaze. I had assumed that we had survived the earlier episode of his apparent dismay at the absence of my virginity and convinced myself that such matters belonged firmly to the past. Evidently not, though, for Arash was now anxious to establish a detailed inventory and comprehensive checklist of my sexual past.

'Just tell me', he snapped impatiently. 'How many were there? One, two ….ten or more? I need to know.'

He then produced a small, ivory-coloured jewellery box. My jewellery box. 'Let's go through these items right now and see what we can find.' I looked on as he carefully picked out a filigree gold necklace and held it up towards me. 'Who gave you this and why?' my inquisitor enquired. His fingers then rifled through a modest collection of pendants, rings, bracelets and brooches, all the time moving quickly on from one item to the next, as if to avoid contamination. Opening out his hands, he looked at me and said 'it's all dirty, you know, dirty and tainted, and I won't allow you to keep any of it in the house.' I looked at Arash stunned by his sordid insinuations and the sexually charged nature of his vivid imagination. To make matters worse it was not as if there was anything of substance to confess to. But I immediately concluded that when it came to the issue of my jewellery, that if these few pieces, birthday presents for the most part, were really going to represent an obstacle to our future happiness together, then Arash could dispose of the whole lot right away. When juxtaposed with my love for him, a few items of gold and silver seemed so meaningless and insignificant. In any event, he appeared to have found a solution of his own. 'You'll never see this again,' he announced. 'I'm donating it all to charity'.

Was this an act of Christian compassion and forgiveness on his part? Certainly not. Or was Arash fulfilling one of the five duties incumbent on every Muslim - that of *Zakāt* - the practice of giving charitably based on accumulated wealth for those who are able? Possibly so. Whatever the case, one of the beauties of the world's great religious texts - from the Ancient Greek scriptures to Zoroastrianism, and just about everything else alphabetically in between, is that there is something for everybody to be found within them, that they are capable of interpretation in a wide variety of often contradictory ways. Of course the Koran, the central religious text of Islam, is no exception in this regard, as Arash's mother, Shahin, knew very well. My prospective mother-in-law never had any issue with my being from another faith - or if she did she made a good job of keeping any reservations to herself. She also happened to be familiar with many of the holy book's 114 chapters - which was why it did not take her too long to read of the four conditions to be satisfied in order for there to be a valid marriage contract: that there should be a clear proposal, at least two competent witnesses, an unambiguous acceptance and a marriage gift by the bridegroom to the bride. There was no mention of any obligation to register the marriage with the relevant civic authorities. Islam, considered by some to be harsh and unbending, in fact seemed to be rather flexible and accommodating - for there was no mention of any obligation for a marriage ceremony to take place within the confines of a mosque - nor even of the necessity for an Imam or Mullah to oversee or conduct the proceedings. And there was further good news. That although Muslim men are not generally permitted to marry non-Muslim women, an exception existed for them to be able to wed what the Koran referred to as 'people of the Book' - a reference to Jews and Christians alike - on the grounds that all three faiths believe in a single God and in revealed scriptures. The children of any such inter-faith union were always to be raised in the faith of Islam, true enough, but Shahin wisely concluded that such a bridge could be crossed in due course.

'*Arash-jaan, Arash-jaan-negah kon! Arash dear - look!*' She could hardly wait to announce the news. 'You were looking for a way to marry Clair and thanks to the Koran we have found it. By marrying you here at home, but not registering the marriage with the municipal authorities, you can be considered man and wife.'

Of course the key issue was whether or not my father would buy it. In fact it was not a difficult sell - as soon as he saw that it was merely a home-made religious ceremony and without any consequences relating either to my nationality or citizenship - well, he had resigned himself to going along with it.

The wedding preparations could now proceed.   Once the date and time had been agreed, it was not long before delicately inscribed invitations, designed and drawn by Arash, were being delivered by hand into an assortment of letter boxes around Tehran - to family, friends and company members for the most part. With my parents due to return to London the following week, time was at a premium. Although anxious to assist Shahin in any way, the discussions relating to the wedding arrangements were rather stilted and awkward. Determined to keep a low profile, Arash's father Parviz had nevertheless agreed that the ceremony and party be held at his house, where Shahin, together with her three daughters and Mansoureh would oversee the catering. Babak was given the task of helping out with decorating the house, whilst Shideh patiently accompanied my mother and I on a mission to find an appropriate dress for the occasion. That proved to be a not particularly taxing task, on the grounds that she already had a specific shop in mind. Her choice of boutique happened to be exactly to my taste, for the outfits there were particularly beautiful. As I looked through the collection, a full length lace dress caught my eye. 'I love that dress too Clair', my mother said, 'try it on'.   Helping me with the hooks and eyes, the sales lady, clearly impatient for my small delegation to observe me in the dress, opened the curtains of the changing room with a grand flourish. After a moment's pause, my mother commented 'oh, it really is beautiful, darling, I love the strapless neckline, it looks really elegant on you'. 'Yes, it does', Shideh agreed, 'and the beige is simple and romantic at the same time - I'm sure my brother will love you in it'. The keen sales lady, sensing our interest in the garment, tried her luck with a matching shoulder wrap , demonstrating it with a coquetish turn. All that was required was a minor alteration to the length of the dress - and we left the shop with both wedding gown and shoulder wrap in tow, congratulating ourselves on a job well done.

I knew that I had a lot to thank my parents for. It was all too easy to get carried away with the detail of the wedding preparations and easier still to overlook the sadness I knew my father was doing his best to conceal under his stoic smile. So I made a point of spending time alone with them in their hotel room. I loved them both so much and now, suddenly, away from Banafsheh street and in the quiet of their room, I suddenly felt a wave of nerves overwhelming me. Closing my eyes I tried to ignore any feelings of uncertainty, edging myself closer to my father as I did so. I placed my head on his shoulder, exactly as I used to as a child when feeling uneasy or scared. As usual he was able sense what was going on in my mind.

'Don't worry, darling, these worries, they are all quite normal, it's just a case of last minute nerves. I remember feeling the same way just before I married your mother.' I knew he was trying to lighten the atmosphere but behind his reassuring words it wasn't difficult to see his underlying sorrow, convinced that he was on the verge of losing his daughter to a man whom he didn't particularly like or approve of, abandoning her in a far and distant land.

Bursts of joyous laughter, quick chatter, the clanging of plates and the rushing of feet up and down steps, all merged to create a most energetic and excited atmosphere in the Alizadeh household. It was October 1973. Preparations were well underway. Typically efficient and understated, Shahin oversaw the transformation of her house on our wedding day. Large vases of honeysuckle and roses adorned every corner of the entrance hall and lounge, filling the air with a heady scent. Sholeh, the youngest of the three sisters, blessed with her mother's kindness and wisdom, was determined to take me into her charge to guide me through the rituals and routines befitting an Iranian bride. With toiletry bags in hand she whisked me away to my first experience of a *hammam*, the Middle Eastern variant of a steam bath. Standing in the humid high-ceilinged cubicles, we set about scrubbing ourselves down with a loofa. Lathering gently all over we stood for a brief moment breathing in the aroma of the rose-scented soap. Once back at her Banafsheh Street home, shortly to become mine too, she plucked my eye-brows, shaped and manicured my nails and with a natural flair, massaged my back and shoulders to relax me for the impending ceremony. For a moment I lay with my eyes shut tight, feeling perfectly pampered. As I put on my wedding dress, I felt exquisitely feminine, the beige silky material flowing around my body and caressing my skin. Carefully placing a string of pearls around my neck and a garland of flowers on my richly hennaed auburn hair, I could hardly believe that this, at last, was my wedding day. Long-awaited and fraught undoubtedly. I wished that my parents had been more eager participants, basking in my joy, rather than being such reluctant recruits to the ceremonial proceedings about to unfold. It was Arash's wish that he too would receive his father's seal of approval but for the moment at least, Parviz was nowhere to be seen. Still, it was my wedding day all the same and my eyes remained firmly focussed on the man who would shortly become my husband.

His face radiated a gentle pride. Arash's perfectly pressed dark brown suit and cream tie were well-chosen and flattered his tall frame. I had only ever seen him in jeans and casual clothes, his immaculate attire prompting me to stop in my tracks for a brief moment as I soaked up the sight of the fine-looking man to whom I would shortly be wed. There was an atmosphere of excitement and expectation as the small number of guests and family members - there were only around twenty of us all told - waited for the marriage ceremony to get underway. Arash and I stood side by side, our sense of relief almost palpable. I thought of the many obstacles we had managed to overcome, the hoops we had been obliged to jump through. My father stood directly opposite us, solemn and dignified. Standing next to my mother, he had volunteered to conduct the proceedings himself. His background and training was as a mechanical engineer - not a Mullah. And yet he took to his new role of interpreting marriage as defined within Islam with an air of confidence and easy expertise, as if he had presided over many such interfaith occasions. 'Has there been a clear proposal of marriage?' he enquired of the man about to become his son-in-law.

'Yes, there has', Arash replied.

My father then turned towards me.

'And do you, Clair, my daughter' - he looked directly at me - 'do you, clearly and unambiguously accept Arash to be your husband?'

I heard myself answer affirmatively, but it was as if my voice came from some distance away.

'I do. I most certainly do.'

Duke then turned his attention to those present in the lounge. His voice now slightly strained, he continued.

'We are privileged to be surrounded by such generous family and friends, here today to share in this happy moment but also serving as witnesses to the joining in matrimony of Clair Symonds and Arash Alizadeh.' With those words Shahin stepped forward, presenting me with a family heirloom, a turquoise ring set in an ornate gold leaf setting.

My father then reverted to a more classical script.

'Since the conditions required for a valid contract of marriage have been met, I now declare you man and wife.' There was cheering, clapping - conviviality and celebration spontaneously breaking out in the lounge - whereupon the wedding party got underway.

Some six hours later, as the last guests were preparing to leave the Alizadehs' residence in Banafsheh Street, and the celebrations began to come to a close, I reflected on the day's proceedings. Of course I was happy - overjoyed, in fact - because I had got what I wanted. Arash and I were now officially man and wife, living together from then on at his parents' home and recognised as a married couple by both families. But I knew very well that my father had suffered considerably throughout the day. It would have been his preference to see me standing under the *chuppah*, the traditional Jewish wedding canopy, marrying a Jewish groom in a ceremony performed by a Rabbi, witnessing the breaking of the glass underfoot and hearing joyous cries of *mazeltov!* ringing out in a synagogue according to time-honoured Jewish tradition. Instead he had been reading passages from the Koran, marrying his daughter off to an Iranian Muslim of whom he thoroughly disapproved - his sole consolation that I was able to retain the British passport which had become so precious to him.

But Duke was not the only disgruntled parent on my wedding day. Arash's father Parviz had not articulated his disapproval in any way. Yet his absence at our marriage sent out a message that could hardly have been more clear. As we danced and partied the evening away in the lounge downstairs, he had remained alone in his bedroom on the first floor, as he had done throughout the day, refusing to have anything to do with the most unusual matrimonial proceedings taking place in his home. Duke and Parviz had hardly spoken two words to one another - but they had come to share the common ground of disapproval, though manifesting it in different ways. Our married life, it seemed, had got off to a distinctly shaky start. A portent, perhaps, for what was to follow.

A Johannesburg childhood of ballet and theatre,
my mother constantly showing me the way

Together with my brother Michael, under the ever watchful eye of my father

Middle row, fourth on the right, with the short black curly hair. My childhood was spent in my mother's dance studio based in our Johannesburg home

Preparing for the annual Eisteddfods in Johannesburg was an important part of the dance year

My parents - Sheila and 'Duke' Symonds

Performing at Talar Roudaki was always a thrilling experience

Arash in pensive mood

Together with Arash at a wedding in Tehran

Both the Shah and the Shahbanou were anxious to showcase the arts in Iran and where better to do so than at Talar Roudaki

Rehearsing in the studio at Talar Roudaki

*Russian coaching
saw to it that
performances of
Les Sylphides
went down well
with Iranian
audiences*

Dancing to the pulsating beat of Bolero

Performing Les Sylphides

Seldom was any expense spared for Iranian National Ballet company productions

The Iranian National Ballet staged lavish productions of many of the major classics

بالهٔ‌ی‌سیلفیدها ـ بالهٔ‌ی‌شهرزاد

واریاسیون برای هشت نفر

LES SYLPHIDES - SCHEHERAZADE

VARIATION FOR EIGHT

ROUDAKI HALL,   تالار رودکی
JAN. 24-FEB. 1,2-1975   ۱۲،۱۲،۴ بهمن ۱۳۵۳

The Shah and his wife, the Empress Shahbanou were regular visitors to Talar Roudaki.

Together with my sister in law Sholeh and father in law Parviz

My second marriage to Arash - at the registry office of Epping Town Hall, with my parents and brother looking on

The modern Iran of today

Chapter 13: Saadabad Palace, Tehran

Together they made a fine pair - sharing the dubious distinction of being two of the most brutal and repressive dictators in the Middle East. But the murky world of regional geo-politics had seen to it that the Shah of Iran and the President of Syria, Hafez al-Assad, had reason to work together on certain key issues, not least a mutual desire to contain any expansionary ambitions on the part of neighbouring Iraq, with which both countries shared vast and highly porous borders. Besides, they both ran extremely authoritarian regimes where the cult of personality was all-pervasive. Which was why the red carpet was being rolled out on the occasion of an official state visit - one to which I, together with other members of the ballet company, had been invited. In truth it was more of an official summons to provide a private performance at the Shah's glamorous Saadabad Palace, a vast complex of eighteen villa-palaces and brick mansions set in an area of over one hundred hectares, where Iran's self-styled *Light of the Aryans* and *Head of the Warriors* lived in the main building known as the White Palace, the most luxurious environment imaginable in which extravagance and excess were the order of the day.

Nejad Ahmadzadeh, the dour director of the Iranian National Ballet, sat on a long wooden bench in the rehearsal room at Talar Roudaki. The anxious look on his face was not unreasonable given the circumstances - he knew that his position as director of the fledgling company depended on a successful outcome. With just one week to prepare, he ordered company members to give their complete commitment to an agreed programme of *divertissement* - six short dances blending classical ballet with ancient local folkloric movement. One of my roles was as a minstrel in a ballet known as Bijan and Manijeh, inspired by the Persian epic poet Ferdowsi's recounting of Iran's mythical and historical past. Bad tempered and fraught, Mr. Ahmadzadeh oversaw the rehearsals shouting at the dancers to keep time more effectively or be more dramatic with their gestures. Our Russian ballet masters, Inga and Robert Urazgildief, both stars of the legendary Kirov Ballet, could only look on nervously from the side-lines, eager to lend a helping hand but acutely aware that interrupting an over-excited Ahmadzadeh was not a sensible proposition, not least in respect of their own positions, any untimely or unwelcome comment possibly leading to the issue of a pair of one way Aeroflot tickets back to the Soviet Union.

'Make sure you have all of your make-up, costumes and ballet shoes ready for a 9 o' clock meeting here at Talar Roudaki on Sunday.' With the dances finally to our director's satisfaction, he was giving company members a last minute briefing.   Focusing an intense gaze directly at my husband, whose failure to respect punctuality was well known, he entered a heart-felt plea. 'And, please do not be late.   I repeat - do not be late.'

My nerves were on edge that Sunday morning.   I knew, as our director did too, that Arash and good time-keeping were equal and exact opposites.   This was why I had set my rather old fashioned but entirely reliable travelling alarm clock for 7 o' clock that morning. 'Arash', I called out from the front door. Clutching my trusty red Westclox timepiece, I pleaded for him to show some sense of urgency. 'Please, Arash, please, *zood-bash*, *zood-bash* - hurry up, hurry up.' Finally on our way, I casually threw the clock into my ballet bag as we battled through the terrible traffic of Tehran.

One rendezvous, one coach ride and one hour later we pulled up outside the first security check-point of the Saadabad Palace.   The dancers of the company formed a queue, awaiting inspection by a tall and rigid no-nonsense member of the Iranian Imperial Guard, the Shah's personal guard force, easily recognised as such by their salmon coloured insignia.   Unlike other soldiers, an Imperial Guard had to pass a series of tests, one of which was to be able to recite his family's history back twenty three generations from memory alone. When my turn came, I smiled nervously.   Plunging his hand into my open bag, he rummaged through my personal effects.   I waited to be admitted through the turnstile gate and into the lavishly landscaped grounds of the palace, where I caught a glimpse of well-tended lawns, a large lake and rows of cypress trees.   Instead he stared suspiciously at me before marching off towards a small cabin, all the time holding my bag firmly in his grasp, but now slightly raised, as if ready to dispose of it at short notice.   I felt a rush of warmth heading up towards my face.   Mr. Ahmadzadeh looked on nervously.   'Is this yours?' the guard barked out, clutching my red travelling alarm.   Its loud tick seemed exaggerated as he held the offending item up towards me. I nodded that it was. 'You not enter the palace with this.' I took a deep breath. 'Why you have this? How I know there is not electric device attached to it?' Convinced that an explanation relating to Arash's habitual tardiness would leave the guard distinctly unimpressed, I simply stood there, wide eyed and silent. 'I keep the clock here - you have it back when performance finish.' I heard myself exhale with relief as I again took possession of my dance bag and set off to join the others already preparing for the performance in an area allocated as dressing rooms for the day.

The Saadabad Palace was situated in the Shemiran area of Tehran, just three kilometres further to the north from Gholhak where I was now living with Arash and his family. Although the palace complex was first inhabited by Qajar monarchs and the royal family back in the 19th century, the Shah of Iran had only moved there in the 1970s. Or moved back, to be more precise, because his mother, Tadj ol-Molouk Ayrumlu, the Queen consort of Iran, had brought him into the world there, eleven months after the end of the First World War.

Whilst the interior of the palace depicted popular Persian mythology, paintings by European masters were in ample supply. Enormous carpets, mostly woven in the north-western city of Khorassan, covered the floors. The Shah's wife, the Empress Farah Pahlavi, had commissioned and overseen much of the palace's interior décor herself. No doubt influenced by her love of French culture, Louis XIV furniture and French antiques featured prominently - but Art Deco was the main theme throughout.

Mr. Ahmadzadeh informed us that both the Shah and the Syrian President were ready and in place. Immediately we swung into action, interpreting the poetry and fables of the Persian poet Omar Khayyám with elegance and ease, aware that amongst us were the rightful heirs to a tradition going back almost one thousand years. Moving seductively to Iranian music, kneeling to face one another in a semi-circle, low bodices revealing bare midriffs and oriental style loose trousers tapered in around the ankles, we resembled the privileged sultanas of an exotic harem, our heavily made up, flashing eyes looking into imaginary mirrors and defying anyone - Shahs and Presidents included - to resist such temptation.

As we took our final curtsies and bows it was satisfying to see a contented smile on the face of his Imperial Majesty. His distinguished guest sat next to him perfectly still, hands clasped firmly together, his upright frame hinting at the background of a military man. Impeccably dressed in a dark blue suit, Mr. Ahmadzadeh stood stiffly to the side, beads of perspiration on his brow, his eyes darting furtively from dancers to the Shah, from Shah to President and then back to his dancers again. As it emerged that the *divertissement* programme had been well received, we were ushered off to another room and told to stand in line, our reward to shake hands with the heads of state of Iran and Syria, the former a friend of Israel, the latter its implacable foe, but both regimes infected with rampant anti-Semitism. And there before them stood a Jewish girl, albeit one whose religious background and identity was destined to remain concealed.

In one of the vast chandeliered rooms of the palace we were then served tea in delicate gold rimmed porcelain cups, accompanied by canapés of caviar, white nougat and a variety of *Shahlai khoshk*, dry Persian pastries. Reluctant to relinquish such pampering and privilege we had to be gently encouraged to take our leave, bags in hand, and out through the turnstile gates. Just as I was boarding the bus for the return journey to Talar Roudaki, I felt a firm tapping on my shoulder.

'Here, *khanoum*, here madam'. It was the surly guard from the gate. 'Here, your clock'. He handed it to me in a brown paper bag. 'That clock never problem for you again'. It was true. Of course I don't know the precise nature of any tests it had been subjected to back in the Imperial guard's cabin. But my little red travelling alarm would never show any sign of life ever again.

Chapter 14: Banafsheh Street, Tehran

Number 61 Banafsheh Street, Gholhak, Tehran - not just my new address - but home. Its heart and soul was undoubtedly the kitchen - Mansoureh and Shahin's domain. Every morning the happy, high-pitched voice of Mansoureh could be heard reverberating around the house as she set about preparing the day's food. When my sister-in-law Shideh - the middle of the three sisters - was in full flow she would entertain the family at the evening meal with her mischievous humour and natural story telling ability, laughter bursting out intermittently from the nine of us seated around the large kitchen table. I would take my usual place next to Arash, trying to catch a word or two of Shideh's anecdotes, my eyes always fixed intently on her expressive face, but unable to decipher anything other than the most elementary phrase.

If there was going to be any communication between us, I had to master the basics of Farsi - and fast. Sholeh took me under her wing, not for the first time, and taught me the numbers. But what a battle just to get to ten.

'Okay, Clair', she said, with her usual warmth and confidence, 'well done - now - *yek boos bedeh*'. That one I happened to know already - '*give me a kiss*', as we burst out laughing together. Aware that I required a more structured environment, I enrolled on a course at the University of Tehran. The University's motto - *Rest not a moment from Learning* - seemed entirely appropriate for the linguistic challenges before me, as I attempted to familiarise myself with an alien system of writing known as Perso-Arabic script. I soon discovered that this included six vowels, twenty-three consonants and a system of grammar that uses derivational agglutination to form new words from nouns, adjectives and verbal stems. Of course I had not the faintest idea what any of that meant - but was left with little choice other than to battle on.

By *Nowruz* of 1974, the day marking the traditional Iranian New Year, I had been living in Iran for some eighteen months, six of them in my new capacity as a married woman - Mrs. Clair Alizadeh. It was March and the fresh air of spring lifted my spirits after the cold winter months.   Every *Nowruz* the Alizadeh family, of which I was now part, would don their smartest clothes and set off to visit elderly relatives - that year it was the turn of my father-in-law Parviz's octogenarian sister.   Shahla, the eldest of the sisters, explained to me that her aunt was a fiercely independent woman who steadfastly refused to accept any offer of help.   She received us warmly in her impeccably clean large home, a half hour's drive to the west of Tehran.   Everything was spotless - from the heavy curtains hanging in the lounge to the highly-polished red apples set out in an orderly fashion in a cut-glass oval-shaped bowl.   Although clearly delighted to see us, she had other matters on her mind that day, anxious not to miss the New Year's message from the Shah.   Glancing at her watch, she rushed to switch on an old Ekco radio-set, one that gave the impression of having served her well for a good half-century or more. Once on the airwaves, it did not take the Shah long to get into his stride.   The story of Pahlavi rule was, he said, '*a saga as bright as Iran's sky*'.   She looked across the room towards her brother, nodding her head gently forward with approval.   '*Today, on the 2533rd Imperial Nowruz, in the name of the standard-bearer of the Iranian monarchy, I hereby renew the eternal covenant of the Pahlavi Dynasty with my nation.*'   I noticed Arash having the opposite reaction, almost physically recoiling at what he had heard, but he had the good sense to hold his tongue.   The implication of the broadcast was clear enough - the Pahlavis were likely to be around for some time to come.   How else to explain that His Imperial Highness, the Crown Prince Reza Pahlavi, just fourteen years old, was already being groomed for the succession?   Just a few years older than my brother-in-law Babak, in fact, who was by now anxious to return home.   Then, as if she had been able to read her nephew's mind with great clarity, the elderly aunt called him over to her side, slipped a few *rials* into his hand by way of a *Nowruz* treat, kissed him gently on each cheek, before bidding us all a heartfelt *motehshakeram* and *khoda-hafez* - thank you and goodbye.   Duty had been done.   We could all now return home.

No doubt my understanding of Islam was superficial and incomplete, but I found learning about the Five Pillars of Islam considerably easier to comprehend than grappling with the intricacies of Farsi.   I discovered that *Zakāt* or alms-giving is but one of the five duties incumbent on every Muslim.   Yet my generous mother-in-law Shahin went well beyond what was required of her in the Koran through voluntary acts of charity known as *sadaqah*.

With Mansoureh and Sholeh assisting her in the kitchen, huge quantities of chicken, meat stew and rice would be prepared in large pots and pans, only then to be loaded into the family's car. I was curious to know what was happening. 'When Arash was very young, perhaps just five or six,' Sholeh explained, tying back her long brown hair into a thick plait, 'he became ill with pneumonia - my mother was extremely worried - she thought he might die.' I listened intently as she continued. 'She prayed hard at that time, vowing that should Arash pull through she would give thanks to Allah for saving his life and provide food for the poor every year thereafter. That was over twenty years ago. Not once did she forget her sacred promise.'

That Shahin should have kept her word did not surprise me. I had already witnessed her generosity myself when she had opened her door to a beggar, immediately inviting him into the house for tea and serving him with food. I had never seen such goodness or generosity of spirit in either Johannesburg or London. I loved my new family. For Shahin I had become a fourth daughter. We might not have been able to chat together very easily but that did not prevent her from being intuitively sensitive to the growing undercurrent of disappointment and sadness I was beginning to experience in terms of my relationship with her son.

'Okay Clair, I'm going out now, I'll see you later.' Here was Arash's constant refrain, one with which I had already become all too familiar, one which I had come to dread. I also knew from his tone that his mind was made up. Of course he had not the slightest intention of allowing me to accompany him.

'Let's go out together Arash. I'll come with you tonight', I would plead. 'Sorry but you can't come Clair.' In truth I hadn't expected any other answer. 'I'll be with a few friends discussing politics, it won't be interesting for you at all'. In some respects what he said was true. Only he could identify and interpret the whispers, the political undercurrent simmering in the back streets, beckoning him into the secretive shadows of houses in which meetings would take place behind closed doors. I knew perfectly well that Arash needed to be involved, to be part of the debate, to discuss matters arduously with like minded friends. I didn't object to that. On the contrary, I was proud of him for being a critic of the Shah's regime. Still, he could see the disappointment on my face at the prospect of being left alone. 'You wouldn't understand anything anyway - you would sit there on your own and be bored.' I didn't mind any of that - I simply wanted to be with the man I loved. Grabbing hold of his denim jacket I knew that there was nothing I could do or say to impede his exit. It wasn't as if he was pursuing another woman - merely ideas. Whatever the case I knew that my husband had no intention of returning home early. He never did. 'Don't worry, I won't be long.' And with that he would leave. I felt desperately sad to see him walk out of the house and then hear the engine of his Mini Moke revving up, preparing to go. Within a few seconds he was gone. Again.

Shahin witnessed the unfolding of this scene many times. Although she never interfered in our marital squabbles, we shared much common ground - sleep would elude us both until Arash had returned home safely. She too struggled to understand her first-born. Whilst she knew that life was difficult for many people in Iran, she failed to understand why her son had to take the weight of their misery onto his shoulders. She worried that he had become too thin of late, was often moody and distant, but her main concern that dabbling in politics in Iran was the equivalent of playing with fire. Why could he not just settle down, finish his degree, and consider purchasing a small apartment in which he could start enjoying life with his young wife? She thought back to how Parviz had conducted himself years earlier: unlike their son he had refused to marry until he could afford to look after his wife and would be able to support a family.

Eventually I would beat a lonely retreat to our bed where I would lie upset and agitated, hour after hour, unable to sleep, watching the clock go well beyond midnight and into the early morning hours. And then, finally, in the distance, there it was - the distinct noise of the Mini Moke - I could recognise it right away, making its way home. I would continue to lie there quite still, saying nothing, but with my eyes wide open, watching Arash undress clumsily before falling into bed.

'I'm still awake Arash', I would inform him. 'I've been waiting up for you for hours.' His clothes would be impregnated with the acrid smell of cigarettes, his breath reeking of alcohol. I was not sure if he could hear me or cared at all. All I knew was that within moments he would have fallen into a deep drunken sleep, breathing heavily to compound my misery. Furious, I would kick him under the bedcovers to wake him up. 'What is it, what is it?' I could feel my throat tighten. 'Arash,' I whispered. 'You're late and drunk again. You've just dropped into bed without so much as an apology and you dare to ask me what's wrong?' Speaking as softly as I could manage in my anguished state, I would begin to vent my wrath - 'well, I'll tell you exactly what it is...' But before I could finish my sentence, Arash would have rushed out of bed, heading urgently to the toilet, where he would cough, splutter and finally vomit out a good deal of the contents, all that had been consumed earlier that evening. Clambering back to the bedroom, holding on to the walls to steady his wobbly legs, he would fall back into bed and instantly to sleep again. I knew there was nothing more to be said. The only thing of which I could be sure was that sleep would continue to elude me. Whatever had happened to my Iranian knight?

It was not without some irony that it should have been during this period of marital stress that my relationship with my father-in-law Parviz began to improve. I had never understood why he had chosen to boycott his son's wedding day, when he had so conspicuously gone out of his way to register his disapproval by absenting himself from the matrimonial proceedings, sulking in his room all day. Was it because he had planned an Iranian bride and more traditional celebrations for his first born son? Or was it because he gave a resounding thumbs-down to Arash marrying a Jew? I really did not know because nothing was ever said. Still, with the passage of time we came to accommodate one another and through daily contact feelings of affection and mutual respect grew between us.

But my Jewishness remained a delicate issue. Certainly it was nothing to be shouted about from the roof tops of Tehran. Quite the contrary. When a close friend of the family, Soheila, popped in for a chat and a cup of tea on one occasion, Shahin spoke up for me, before I had time to formulate my own response. The conversation had turned to the

Hajj, the pilgrimage during the Islamic month of *Dhu al-Hijjah*, when every able-bodied Iranian Muslim who could afford it should undertake the two thousand kilometre journey to Mecca. It was the fifth and final Pillar of Islam, the pilgrimage meant to be undertaken at least once in every Muslim's lifetime. Soheila turned to me, her tone kindly and inquisitive. 'Clair *khanum* - Clair, my dear - what exactly is your faith?' Shahin was immediately on her guard. I had never been asked such a direct question about my religion before, at least not in Iran, and I was a little taken aback. But before I could prepare an appropriate reply - of course I did not know how to translate 'Jewish' into Farsi - Shahin had replied on my behalf. 'Christian,' Shahin said, with not the slightest hesitation. 'Clair is Christian.' I nodded and gave a sweet smile. I had neither the confidence nor the linguistic skills to contradict my mother-in-law, least of all in front of her friend. But later that day I regretted not having spoken up, ashamed for in effect colluding with the notion that being Jewish was somehow our little secret, something best not mentioned, my religion to be hushed up at all times. And so my life as an unlikely Christian continued the following Christmas, with Shideh and Sholeh thoughtfully going out of their way to prepare a small tree in my honour. Not as part of an elaborate ploy to disguise my religious background but because they believed that 'the Festive Season' was part and parcel of western culture, no matter what your faith. Decorated with holly, brightly coloured tinsel and a large illuminated star placed carefully at the top - the Star of Bethlehem from the Nativity - we would pop back and forth to the Grand Bazaar buying presents to offer one another come Christmas day.

As the year of 1975 drew to a close, I took a step back to look at what had become of me - a Jewish girl living with her in-laws in Tehran whose marriage was under strain and where, to make matters easier for one and all, I went along with being passed off as a Christian, dispensing with the ancient rites and rituals of my own Jewish faith.

Chapter 15: Mansoureh

I was fascinated to learn about Mansoureh's life, of the circumstances of her arrival at the Alizadeh residence in Banafsheh Street, Tehran. Fortunately, Shahin was at hand to satisfy my curiosity. It was back in the early sixties, a good decade before I had set foot in Iran. As she described Mansoureh's journey from the Iranian countryside to a metropolitan life Tehran, it reminded me of Richard's arrival at St John's Road, Johannesburg, the setting of my early, formative years in South Africa. Mansoureh and Richard were of a similar age, both were from poor and remote rural locations, both had been seeking employment as domestic staff and unbeknown to them at the time, both were poised to embark on experiences that would change them for all time. Richard was a servant, an innocent victim of apartheid with an absence of any democratic rights. Of course Mansoureh was not. And yet their everyday lot seemed to me to share much common ground. I sat in the kitchen and listened with great interest to Shahin telling the tale of the shy young teenage girl standing at her front door next to her father, a threadbare scarf covering her loosely tied brown hair, a clean tee-shirt tucked neatly in at her thin waist, with large tired dark eyes looking up cautiously towards her prospective employer. To my delight I was understanding much of my mother-in-law's Farsi. '*Befarmeh, befarmeh* - please, please,' Shahin had said, 'you must come in and have something to eat and drink.'

'*Kheili motchakeram khanoum* - thank you so much Madam', Mansoureh's father had replied, looking down towards the ground. The twin themes of his life to date had been those of poverty and hardship, as he explained that his family lived in a run-down, ramshackle, one-roomed house where there was neither electricity nor running water. Just like Richard, I thought.

'*Agha khan* - my dear Sir', Shahin had said respectfully, 'we will take Mansoureh into our home with pleasure. You have my word that I will look after her as if she were one of my daughters.'

The father had looked at Shahin, his small face burnt from years of hard physical labour under the scorching sun, his eyes full of anguished gratitude. 'You have been very kind to our family.

Mansoureh will be happy to help in your home. She is a good girl and will be much missed, especially by her mother, but we have been left with no choice other than to part with her.'

As Shahin offered the young girl orange juice and *nan-e gerdui*, traditional walnut biscuits, she enquired if there were any particular issues of which she should be aware.

'Yes', the father had replied. 'There are no hospitals or doctors near our village and my daughter needs medical help. We didn't pay much attention to it at first, but when Mansoureh started losing her hair, we thought it would grow back in time. But it hasn't. That's why she wears that scarf all the time now - she is bald around the crown of her head.' A proud man, he struggled to hide the emotion in his voice. 'Perhaps the doctors here in Tehran might be able to help her.' Kissing her on each cheek, he set off from the Alizadehs' house on the long journey home. He was clearly lost in his own thoughts, wondering how long it would be before he would see his daughter again.

Just three years my senior, Mansoureh had been one of those present on my wedding day. She had indeed become part of the family, precisely as Shahin had promised. But what of her own hopes of marriage? By now 25 years old, she was already running rather late according to the traditional but unspoken Iranian timeline which framed her life. She was terribly discrete, giving little away in that regard. Not that Mansoureh had in any way been inactive in the pursuit of romance. For the signs were there for all to see.

Her voice would reverberate throughout the house. '*Khoda-hafez khanum* - bye bye.' Throwing a brightly coloured *chador* over her head, she was off to the shoemaker - and not for the first time that week. Or the week before. Undeterred by the absence of any shoes requiring repair, she found one of Arash's boots and persuaded herself that it would benefit from a new heel. Whereupon she would begin the ten-minute walk, the real purpose of which was to spend a few moments with Fereydoon, the young shoemaker to whom she had given her heart. Mansoureh's regular sorties had not gone unnoticed by Shahin who took it upon herself to broach the subject. Sitting

110

together at the kitchen table, separating the leaves from a large bunch of strongly-scented mint, Shahin set about her task.

'And how is *agha* Fereydoon the shoe-maker keeping these days?' she enquired, her eyes remaining firmly focused on the process in hand. Mansoureh looked at Shahin.

'*Khanum*', she said confidently, 'he is very good, and he looks at me kindly. You've seen him. Don't you think that he is a very nice looking man? I can't tell for sure - but I think he likes me too.'

'*Mansoureh*', Shahin replied. 'I have had news from your father.' Mansoureh knew right away that this could mean only one thing - an arranged marriage. She sat frozen to her chair waiting for the bad news. 'He has decided that you are to be married to Saeed, a young man from a good family. He is also from your village.'

'*Khanum*', Mansoureh replied, the desperation in her voice not difficult to detect. 'Madam, I have been away from my village for over ten years now. That is not my place anymore. I have learned new ways and new ideas - I wouldn't be right with anyone from my village.' Shahin agreed that it would be a retrograde step. But she also knew that the wishes of Mansoureh's father had to be respected. Might she be able to make the match sound any more appealing?
'Saeed works in Tehran as a delivery man. So at least you would be able to stay here in the capital'.

Mansoureh knew that the time for playing games was over. She decided there and then to reveal her true feelings.

'I can't, *khanum*. I have fallen in love with agha Fereydoon.' She paused for a few seconds before gathering the courage to continue. 'I would like Fereydoon - not Saeed - to be my husband.' And just to ensure that there could be no misunderstanding, she repeated the shoemaker's name. 'Fereydoon'.

Aware that she was asking for trouble by siding with Mansoureh, Shahin put her hand on her shoulder and replied gently. 'I will pay Fereydoon a visit and see what I can do.'

Jumping off her chair, Mansoureh flung her arms around Shahin, her eyes filled with joy. 'Thank you, thank you *khanum*', she cried out. Twirling around the kitchen table, clicking her fingers high in the air, she immediately pictured herself in a beautiful white wedding dress and veil staring into the ceremonial mirror. But Mansoureh's joy would prove to be short-lived. For just a few days later Shahin returned to the house bearing bad news.

'I am very sorry Mansoureh. But *agha* Fereydoon doesn't want to marry you. He doesn't want to marry anyone. At least not until he is in a better financial position. He apologises if he misled you in any way. He is very sorry and wishes you well'. Mansoureh stood there silently. It had taken no more than a few seconds to shatter her dreams.

Chapter 16: The Black Swan of the Iranian National Ballet?

Perhaps there should never have been an Iranian National Ballet Company in the first place - emulating a western style of dance which takes its inspiration from the courts of the Italian Renaissance. Perhaps it would have been more appropriate to have a company devoted entirely to Persian dance - something more authentic, more eastern - in keeping with the time-honoured traditions of Iran. Where intricate hand motions, elaborate hip movements and coquettish glances at the audience were the order of the day rather than formalised movement, mime and acting set to music, the hallmarks of classical ballet. But no such company existed. Or rather existed no longer. In this respect the Iranian National Ballet had come to reflect the prevailing ethos of Iran's ruling elite in the 1970s, its enthusiasm to embrace western culture in general and American culture in particular continuing to proceed at a fast and furious pace. My place of work had become a microcosm of Iranian society, in a sense, a snapshot of what was happening elsewhere in the country. The ballet company's main patron was no less a figure than Her Imperial Majesty the Shahbanou, who saw to it that there was an endless supply of funds, Savak agents from her husband's much-feared secret police force would go about their sordid business unimpeded within the confines of Talar Roudaki and, mirroring what happened as a matter of course within the upper echelons of government, corruption and nepotism were similarly the order of the day. On one occasion I happened to get a glimpse of financial malpractice myself - but being young and naïve I made the mistake of not holding my tongue.

Once a month I would make my way to the administrative offices of Talar Roudaki in order to collect my salary. Payments were always in cash. A plain manila envelope would be handed over and I would enter my signature into the appropriate column of a ledger book to confirm the sum of *rials* received. But more often than not the amount signed for and the money in the envelope did not tally. Arash had warned me to be on the look out for such unscrupulous behaviour - it seemed as though young foreign company members were easy pickings - since I was not the only dancer whose pay was being docked for no apparent reason. What began as a minor niggle soon developed into a growing sense of outrage.

The recreation area was full of tired dancers resting their aching muscles after a particularly demanding ninety minute morning class given by our teachers Inga and Robert. The air was thick with the smell of cigarette smoke and coffee. With rehearsals for a lavish production of the Tchaikovsky classic Swan Lake due to get underway, I was happy with my role as one of the four Little Swans. Then I saw him, Mr. Ahmadzadeh, puffed up with his own importance, the man who for me had come to personify all that was corrupt not just with the ballet company but in Iran as a whole. I had been mulling over what it was I should say. Fired up, I was waiting for the right moment to strike. I thought I would lead him into a trap, informing him in a matter of fact manner that I had just returned from the accounts office where I had collected my salary. 'Good', he said, his arms rising up in a grand gesture of approval.

'No, Mr. Ahmadzadeh, no', I heard myself say. 'It wasn't good at all.' I noticed the smile fading quickly from his face. 'What do you mean Clair, what's the matter?'

He might not have been beside me, but I could hear Arash's voice propelling me on. 'There was money missing from my pay packet Mr. Ahmadzadeh', the sudden silence of those around me immediately apparent. I felt confident that some of the other dancers would show some sympathy or lend their support. But they did not. The company's director moved his head back slightly, as if the notion of my trimmed down pay-packet had come as a complete surprise.

'Let's go to my office Clair. We can discuss the matter there.' But no, that wasn't good enough. I decided to take it upon myself to show him up for what he was - there and then in front of the assembled gathering of dancers, musicians and administrative staff alike.

'Well, I am perfectly happy to stay right here - I certainly don't have anything to hide.' Whereupon I threw caution to the wind. I looked directly into his eyes, defying him to answer with absolute honesty. 'Well, do you? Do you not take our money and line your own pocket with it Mr. Ahmadzadeh?' Before the words were out of my mouth I knew I had spoken out of turn. But there was nothing I could do to retract what had been said. Immediately I was summonsed to the director's office.   It did not take long for the consequences of my ill-thought accusations to become apparent.   I was fired on the spot.

I don't know what possessed me to speak my mind so freely that day. Crossing swords with Mr. Ahmadzadeh, and in public to boot, was manifestly not a good idea - a duel in which I was surely doomed from the outset.   But the genie was out of the bottle and now, sadly, I was out of Talar Roudaki.   One unexpected but beneficial by-product of my solitary protest was that once home Arash came to comfort me. He was proud that I had taken a stand.   Through speaking up for my own rights, he said, I was by definition fighting for the rights of others. The family were similarly outraged by my dismissal and accepted that the foreign dancers were more vulnerable and, as such, less likely to strike back against unethical behaviour.   'Clair *jaan*', my sister in law Shahla enquired calmly, 'what will you do now?'   Needless to say I was unable to come up with a compelling response - the truth was that there had been a lack of synchronicity between my brain and my mouth and I hadn't yet had the time to clearly think the consequences of the entire debacle.   'We shall fight this together', Arash informed Shahla.   His words might well have been sincere but both Shahla and I knew that they were unlikely to yield anything positive in terms of my being reinstated.

The days began to pass slowly.   The weeks began to drag.   As I watched Arash set off for work in the mornings, I longed to be able to accompany him to Talar Roudaki.   During the day I would look at the clock almost obsessively, wondering what he might be doing at that precise moment.   Worst of all was that my body was beginning to feel unworked and sluggish.   I knew precisely the remedy: to take class.   I became desperate to feel my muscles working again, to hear the piano music, to run and spin and jump, to become sweaty and exhausted, to inhale the atmosphere of rehearsal rooms and the theatre where I could gossip with Ros and Maggie - all of which had evidently become part and parcel of my being.   I missed the precision of pirouettes, the energy of *grandes jetées*.   I missed the hauntingly beautiful music of *Swan Lake*.   And when after just two weeks that sense of longing started to turn into a physical ache I knew that the time had come to pay a return visit to Mr. Ahmadzadeh's office where I would, if all went well, eat a large slice of humble pie.

It was almost as if he had been expecting me, as he sat there behind a grand desk.

'Clair', he said, with a large smile on his face. He gave the impression of being happy to see me. I said what I had come to say. That I was sorry. That I had spoken out of turn. That any inconsistencies in accounting were naturally nothing whatsoever to do with him. That my behaviour was inexcusable. And would he please give me another chance. Because he could rest assured that I had learned my lesson. 'Of course I will take you back into the Iranian National Ballet Company'. I breathed a sigh of relief whilst at the same time doing my best to conceal the broad grin about to break out on my face. 'But for the rest of the present contract, Clair, I am afraid that you will have to take a reduction in your salary'. He had won. I had lost. But I really didn't care. I was back, nourishing my body with the nutrition of which it had been temporarily deprived. Ballet - and lots of it. I took my place along side the three other Little Swans, wondering how they had fared without me.

The fourth Little Swan had by now become a great enthusiast of Iranian cuisine, a fact which did not always sit easily with fitting into a ballet tutu. As the mouth-watering aromas of chopped chives, turmeric and black-eyed peas would waft around the house, I knew right away that *qormeh sabzi* was being prepared downstairs in the kitchen, gently simmering away on the stove. I was determined to acquire these culinary skills for myself, especially for this delicious herb stew. It was said by some to be the national dish of Iran, although others would insist that it was *chelo kebab*. That debate did not distress me unduly - I found both equally delicious. More easily said than done to learn the gastronomic tricks of the trade in Iran though - there was never so much as a single cook book in sight. And when I would enquire of Sholeh as to the precise amounts of each ingredient to be used, she would look at me with disbelief, informing me that when it came to Iranian cuisine there were no exact measurements, that everyone had their own particular technique, usually passed down from mother to daughter and thus from one generation to the next.

I was enjoying a moment with Sholeh, already a confident cook in her own right, when Arash came into the kitchen, his aura one of energy and enthusiam. A warm sensation enveloped my body.

'Clair', he said, looking straight at me. It was unusual for him to be giving me his undivided attention whilst in the presence of his sisters.

'Come outside and see what I've bought.' I followed him into the street and immediately saw the object responsible for his uncharacteristically upbeat mood. Parked in pride of place next to his khaki-coloured Mini Moke was a metallic blue motorbike, a Suzuki 125.

'We'll never have problems in the early morning traffic again', he announced with some pride. Brandishing a pair of matching silver helmets, he was determined that we hit the road right away.

I sat nervously behind Arash, clinging tightly to his vest, half closing my eyes or staring intently into his back so as to take my mind away from the reckless drivers all around. But in a surprisingly short space of time, I began to relax my grip, open my eyes, focus on the road and enjoy the sudden bursts of acceleration, as we weaved our way in and out of the traffic. I looked forward to these moments, when I would be able wrap my arms around Arash's slender waist and feel his well defined muscles underneath a light summer shirt. These were rare, precious occasions - just the two of us together. I almost felt guilty, as if involved in some illicit affair, as if stealing time together. For once I was close to him, inhaling heady breaths of his natural scent, yearning for him to drive on and on so that we might really make a life together, one in which I could truly be his wife, away from the always tender but sometimes stifling grasp of his family. It was during those risky rides through the traffic of Tehran that I came to realise that despite four years of marriage in conditions which were far from ideal, I retained a profound love for my husband.

Arash's new motorbike did not go unnoticed by the group of casual workers who would while away the hours chatting or playing backgammon outside the main entrance to Talar Roudaki. His friendly demeanour and relaxed manner made him a popular figure.

'Arash khan, *hale shoma chetoreh*, how are you?' a voice called out from the crowd. I had long since become accustomed to my own presence being ignored. 'Hey, that bike suits you.' 'Biya inja', they called to him, 'come here'. 'Come, you want a cigarette?' Arash waved to them *courteously* as we approached Ali, the eldest of the group of men, who was evidently anxious to have the last word. 'We are all impatient Arash. You have a beautiful young wife and yet you are keeping us all waiting *pedar sukhteh*, you rotten devil.' Arash looked at Ali with an air of curiosity. 'We are waiting for your first born son, of course.'

There seemed to be an air of agreement all round. Certainly there was no dissenting voice. 'And what a good father you would make. I can just see your little boy riding on the back of that bike, holding on to you for dear life.' And with that they burst out laughing. 'A little Arash khan', Ali insisted. 'Sorry, it's too late to chat now, we are running late for work', Arash replied dismissively, 'let's speak tomorrow. Khodahafes, goodbye.' And with those words we made our way up to the rehearsal rooms on the fourth floor. Neither of us spoke in the lift. We both knew that Ali had said precisely what was on my mind. He was right - I was indeed desperate for a little Arash-khan of my own - boy or girl - it really didn't matter to me. But each and every time I had broached the subject, I would receive a similiar answer. 'Clair, you're still so young - just twenty three. And there is your ballet career to think of.' Yet I knew that it was possible to combine motherhood with work. After all Maggie had a little boy of three, remained as slim and fit as ever and was such an integral part of the company that Talar Roudaki would have seemed incomplete without her. 'But most importantly of all', Arash would continue, 'becoming a parent is a huge responsibility. You need far more life experience before bringing another little soul into this world. I am sorry, Clair, but you are really not ready.' Arash had come to influence virtually every aspect of my life - from the development of my knowledge relating to the politics and culture of Iran to being the inspiration behind my short-lived rebellion before the director of the ballet company - and just about everything else in between. I had allowed him to. But now, it seemed, he was in charge of my biological clock as well. Reluctantly, begrudgingly, against my better judgment, I ceded authority to him in that sphere too.

It was as well that my mind had been distracted by the plight of a beautiful princess. Her name was Odette. Her great misfortune was that she had been turned into a swan by von Rothbart, an evil sorcerer. But the good news was that a handsome young Prince had found her at *Swan Lake* and fallen in love with her. What was it that could possibly break the spell and turn Odette back into a princess? Why, only true love of course. As usual with the Iranian National Ballet, no expense had been spared. If the Royal Ballet Company or the *Opéra de Paris* could stage extravagant productions of *Swan Lake*, then we could too. The Shahbanou had been determined that when it came to the performing arts, the message should go out in the Middle East and beyond that Iran was up there in the premier league, an artistic force to be reckoned with. No surprise, then, that with just a day or so to go before opening night, our work schedule should have intensified. Madame Inga oversaw the final rehearsals to ensure that the *corps de ballet* was focused and centred, lines straight, circles quick and fleeting, arms extended to maximum effect, feet pointed to perfection. White ballet tutus with silver sequins had been individually sewn for each dancer, a few feathers delicately placed on tightly pulled back hair. *Pointe* shoes had been carefully worn in, not too soft to trouble us with blistered toes, not too hard to distract the audience with noise from the wooden sprung-floor of the sizeable stage. When finally on opening night the lights dimmed, a hush fell over the audience as we four swans slipped out from behind the curtains to take our places, standing closely in a single line, hands intertwined.

The conductor lifted his baton and nodded gently. Off we went - heads turning to the left with military precision, then to the right, eyes always aligning in the same direction, eight feet operating as if on automatic pilot, performing in perfect harmony. But as the fast footwork continued, I soon began to feel strangely out of sync. And not without some justification. Because as I turned my head sharply to the right, I found myself staring directly into the eyes of the swan on my right. I was in trouble. Four times I stared into the ever widening eyes of the swan next to me, four times I was incapable of correcting my mistake. I was responsible for ruining one of the most famous set-piece dances of *Swan Lake*, designed to showcase synchronised precision ballet. As I prepared to take an entirely undeserved curtsey, I wondered how the audience would express their disapproval.   I learned there and then that Iranian audiences have a mischievous sense of humour - they immediately saw the funny side and burst into spontaneous applause for all four Little Swans who, finally separated, happily sped off stage.

Chapter 17: Pre-Revolutionary Turmoil

Mansoureh handed around some expensive cakes and sweet Iranian pastries to the guests before straightening her scarf and sitting down on a large cane chair close to Shahin. Nervously she looked towards Saeed, the man who had come to ask for her hand in marriage. Sitting uncomfortably in an ill-fitting suit, his deep set dark eyes gave little away. Mansoureh cast her mind back to Fereydoon, sighing quietly to herself as she did so, accepting that any dreams she might have harboured of a love match between herself and the shoemaker now belonged to the past. It was perhaps as well she had moved on, even if her grieving for the shoemaker was not complete, for presents from her future in-laws were in the process of being handed around, wedding arrangements finalised, precisely as Mansoureh's father had intended from the outset.

When, a few weeks later the ceremony was being prepared, a large and richly embroidered cashmere spread was laid out on the floor of the lounge in Banafsheh Street - the very same room in which I too had been wed. Silver candelabras were carefully positioned either side of an ornate mirror, through which Mansoureh, reluctantly resigning herself to her fate, reflected a thin half-smile towards Saeed. Perfumed irises and the delicate scent of rose water filled the room as the ceremony got underway.

True to her promise, Shahin had seen to it that the basement of Banafsheh Street be refitted to accommodate the newly-weds. For a short period of time, a few weeks perhaps, their domestic routine proceeded uneventfully - Mansoureh helping in the home, Saeed going about his delivery rounds in Tehran on an old but reliable dark blue scooter. But soon the sound of Mansoureh's anguished screams could not be ignored, regularly finding their way up the two flights of stairs to where Arash and I had our room. He would immediately rush down to the basement to investigate.

It soon emerged that the small but powerfully built Saeed had thought nothing at all of giving his young wife a good hiding for what he considered her inappropriate dress sense. Although she retained a natural reserve both in terms of her wardrobe and behaviour, this was clearly insufficient to meet with the more stringent requirements of her husband. He was adamant that no part of her legs should be on display, which was why he insisted that she wear trousers underneath her skirt. Mansoureh, no longer used to this stricter code, had stubbornly stood her ground and refused. Having spent the best part of her life in a home where education and middle-class values went hand in hand with a more liberal approach to religion and an overriding respect for human dignity, it was not an unreasonable position to take. But Saeed did not share that view. His take on the situation was quite unambiguous - her duty was to obey.

But now the stakes were considerably higher. Mansoureh was heavily pregnant. As Arash arrived in the basement flat he found her sitting on a large armchair, red with rage. 'He kicked me in the stomach Arash khan', she said between sobs, her hands wrapped protectively around her extended belly. Then she repeated the same phrase, as if in disbelief. 'He kicked me in the stomach Arash khan.' My husband's response was not of much practical use to Mansoureh. 'Oh my God', he exclaimed. Whatever the case, it seemed to be sufficient to give Mansoureh the courage to continue speaking. 'I have never seen a man in this house beat a woman', she said, looking directly at her husband. '*Agha khan* has never hit Shahin *khanoum*, but now my husband is beating me. What have I done that is so bad?' It was the cue for Saeed to enter his plea in mitigation. 'But you know very well, Arash *khan*, that she doesn't listen to me', he shouted. 'She just doesn't listen to me. She is my wife and she will dress as I say'. 'But I haven't worn trousers under my skirt since I left my parents and my village', Mansoureh retorted. 'Tell him, Arash khan, tell him that things are different for women here in Tehran'.

It was clearly a dilemma for Arash. Whilst he didn't want to separate the couple, he knew that the safety of the prospective mother and that of the unborn baby was paramount. 'Listen to me, both of you', he said, weighing his words carefully. 'Mansoureh, you musn't be so obstinate, you have to allow your husband to have his say. Try to find a way that encourages harmony between you both even if that means wearing trousers underneath your skirts and dresses.' 'But Saeed', he continued without a pause, 'I'm sorry, but you will have to leave the house. Go away for a week and think about what you have done. It is not just your wife that you are hurting - you are putting the life of your own baby in danger too. Until you can promise me that you will never strike her again, you will not be welcome back in this house. Do I make myself clear?' Saeed nodded his head in reluctant acquiescence. And as he did so all three parties to the proceedings knew perfectly well that that particular beating would certainly not be her last.

A few months later Mansoureh had done not just what was expected of her but what she had been hoping for too - giving birth to a baby girl - Bahareh, *she who brings Spring flowers*. Of course the Alizadeh women, myself included, immediately took Bahareh into our hearts, although in truth her arrival served only to deepen my longing for a child of my own. Wrapped snugly in a white cotton towel, I looked on longingly wondering when my moment would come. Latching on tightly to Mansoureh's breast and feeding hungrily, Bahareh's eyelids would soon become heavy, her rosebud lips gently easing their grip as she drifted back to sleep.

As the winter of 1976 approached, my fourth in Iran, Saeed decided that it would be appropriate for the family to return to his village, a visit to his parents long overdue. What he really had in mind was to show off Bahareh - and who could blame him for that? Mansoureh went out of her way to ensure that the two hour bus ride to the southwest of Tehran on the road towards the city of Qom, the largest centre for Shi'a scholarship in the world, would go smoothly, preparing sandwiches, soft drinks and fruit which she set out carefully in a multi-coloured carrier bag. She had made a trip to Tehran's Grand Bazaar a few days earlier, purchasing a small brown teddy bear which was now perched in pride of place on top of the other provisions. Her presence seemed to bring a sense of energy to the Alizadeh household and the family home seemed considerably quieter during the periods of her absence. One week later and shortly after their return journey to Tehran was getting under way, the telephone rang in Banafsheh Street, interrupting Shahin's afternoon sewing session as it did so. Slowly she turned to her husband, the blood drained from her face. 'Parviz, there's been a terrible accident! Mansoureh is in hospital.'

The bus driver, whose responsibility it was to bring baby Bahareh and her parents safely back to Tehran, had fallen asleep at the wheel. The vehicle, speeding along the poorly-maintained pot-holed roads, had careered out of control, overturned and left a trail of death and destruction in its wake. As Shahin and Parviz rushed off in their own car to the scene, a rescue team was hard at work attempting to free those unfortunates who remained trapped in the mangled wreckage. Mansoureh had survived and, miraculously, relatively unscathed. But both her husband and daughter had not. Since I was myself devastated at the loss of Bahareh, a baby I had come to love, I could not even begin to imagine the depths of Mansoureh's grief, forced as she was to confront the reality of the most terrible tragedy that had befallen her.

Slowly, during the course of the following weeks and months, the family rallied round and nursed Mansoureh back to good health. Before long she resumed the routine of domestic service and daily chores which had become so familiar to her. It was during this period of recovery and recuperation that she would regularly be informed, as if it were some sort of self-evident truth, that she was *one of the lucky ones*. It was not an opinion which she would ever come to share. Whereas the shoemaker had broken her heart, the loss of her beloved Bahareh in particular had precisely the same effect on her mind, body and soul alike. The once light hearted young girl, with a bubbly spirit and infectious laugh began to withdraw into a world of her own, one inhabited by painful memories and a fading imagery of her beloved Bahareh. Stripped of her *Spring flower* it was hardly surprising that she should have embarked on a slow but steady decline. No, Mansoureh was not one of the lucky ones at all.

It was at this time during the mid-1970s that His Imperial Majesty the Shah had taken it upon himself to abolish Iran's multi-party system of government, the consequence of which was to enable him to rule even more autocratically - and centrally - through his *Hejebh Rastakhis* or Resurrection Party, the only one ever published on electoral lists. Henceforth you were either with the Monarchy or against it. But woe betide should you happen to choose the latter. In fact the Shah was good enough to spell out the consequences very clearly in his own words. Any person deciding not to join his new Resurrection Party

124

was '*either an individual who belongs to an illegal organization or a traitor. Such an individual, if he desires, can leave the country. In fact he can go anywhere he likes, because he is not Iranian, he has no nation*'. Then, a few months later, as if acting out the truth behind the English aristocrat Lord Acton's time-honoured adage that '*all power corrupts; absolute power corrupts absolutely*', the Shah took it upon himself to change the country's calendar from Islamic to Imperial. He decreed that the birth of Cyrus, the first Persian emperor and founder of the Persian Empire, would henceforth be marked as its first day, rather than the flight of the Prophet Muhammad from Mecca to Medina. Overnight, the year changed from 1355 to 2535.

It would be an understatement to say that the Shah's increasingly dictatorial rule, his ill-considered attempts to secularise Iran and quell the country's religious and conservative forces, succeeded in alienating the vast majority of his subjects. But it was always difficult to accurately assess the political climate in Iran - even for Arash - who followed each of these developments with close interest. You might pick up an anti-Shah word or two here and there, especially when chatting with Tehrani taxi drivers, who also reported that there was rising concern amongst the city's clerics and all-powerful *bazarris*. But people were scared to talk openly and freely. And with the prospect of the city's notorious Evin Prison awaiting you - already crammed to bursting point with political prisoners but apparently always happy to receive more - their reluctance to speak out was entirely understandable. Still, if the Shah could not see the writing on the wall nor could the agents of his main political backer, the United States, whose Defense Intelligence Agency would shortly be preparing a detailed briefing for their political masters in Washington, the unambiguous conclusion of which was that the Shah '*is expected to remain actively in power over the next ten years.*'

It sounds a little grand to say so - but the political situation in Iran seemed to impact upon Arash in a most direct way. I remained convinced that his underlying malaise was directly attributable to the oppressive nature of the Shah's regime. So too with all that was wrong in our marriage. The mood swings, his occasional bouts of drunkenness, always keeping me at arm's length - it was all because he found himself trapped within a vicious circle of oppression. I had by now become more than familiar with its geometry. Arash was unable to obtain a passport because he refused to complete his architectural degree. But completing his studies would mean two years compulsory military service - which he steadfastly refused to do. Yet only the completion of military service could lead to the issue of a passport. A vicious circle. As a consequence he felt imprisoned within the borders of Iran, a country he loved but in which he was unable to freely express his opinions, unable to read the literature of his choice but above all unable to leave. Whilst I continued to understand Arash's dilemma - his father did not.

Their constant quarrelling would cast a dark shadow over the house in Banafsheh Street. Sholeh explained to me Parviz's point of view. 'For years now our father has begged Arash to get on with his life. To finish his degree, complete his army training and work in a profession away from the world of ballet.' The fact that Arash would often help friends to complete their own degrees only rubbed salt into the wound. Shaking her head sorrowfully, she continued. 'My father has worked hard all of his life and would not marry until he was sure he could support his wife. My brother is twenty-nine now - but he still relies on our father to provide food and put a roof over his head.' I could hardly spring to Arash's defence quickly enough. 'It must be very frustrating for Parviz - but Arash is deeply unhappy. Once he gets out of Iran he will be a different person and things will improve.' I had become so accustomed to trotting out this protective patter, notably to my own parents, that they had required little modification for me to deliver the same words to my sister-in-law Sholeh.

Mirroring the political changes orchestrated by the Shah, the Iranian National Ballet Company entered a period of transition too. Over the years I had become accustomed to Mr. Ahmadzadeh's loud laugh, heavy gait and roguish smile. We had survived the episode of my firing and rehiring - in truth we had become quite fond of one another. And thanks to the inspirational tuition of our Russian ballet master and mistress, the company had improved beyond all measure. Not only in technical and artistic terms - we had matured, becoming a tightly-knit and coherent ensemble. Then, suddenly, without warning or explanation, Madame Inga and Monsieur Robert were whisked away back to the Soviet Union - their last class a terribly tearful affair. Then came Mr. Ahmadzadeh's own reward for his years of dedication and hard work - he was forced to take early retirement by the powers that be.

Within a few weeks a new Director, Ali Gholampour, had installed himself in Mr. Ahmadzadeh's office.   Although Iranian, he had spent much of his professional life working with American dance companies - a perfect profile for the Iran of the mid-seventies. As he walked into the rehearsal studios for the first time, his straight dark hair covered his ears and it was not difficult to detect a slight smirk on the angular jaw-line of his broad face.   We company members had every reason to stand uneasily that day - he had brought along a group of his own dancers.   Around ten of them - all American.   A new broom had arrived. No crystal ball was required to see what was going to happen - not only would this new group of dancers come to constitute the backbone of the Iranian National Ballet Company - they would soon become its principal dancers too.   Arash had been making the point for years that the Shah was nothing more than a puppet of the United States, a shallow culture rapidly contaminating Iran.   It was a sweeping assertion, admittedly, but one which I had come to accept as a broad general concept.   But I had not for one moment imagined that positive proof of its veracity would one day be standing there in ballet shoes before my own eyes within the well-equipped rehearsal studios of Talar Roudaki.   I knew very well what this meant - trouble.

Chapter 18: Staging an Exit

From time to time, but with growing frequency, Arash would set off from Tehran for a few days. It was my destiny, it seemed, to be kept in the dark as to the precise details of these clandestine outings. All I could glean was that he was due to undergo a series of medical tests. In some respects that was all I needed to know - for I understood that *medical tests* was a euphemism for what he desperately hoped would eventually lead to his being deemed unfit for military service, the issue of a passport and thus a way out of Iran. It was a painfully slow and exasperating business. As he went about attempting to weave a way through cumbersome, corrupt and multi-layered Iranian bureaucracy, his overriding goal was to convince a panel of army doctors and opticians that his eye-sight was simply not good enough to warrant a spell in the army. Easier said than done - he was hardly the first prospective draft-dodger with perfect vision to come knocking on their door. But Arash remained confident that a combination of his acting skills and dogged determination would in due course grind them down. With an overwhelming desire to be as far away as possible from the Shah's regime in Iran, it was as well that he retained such a sense of optimism.

The arrival of Ali Gholampour's American contingent made it abundantly clear that there was now a surplus of dancers at Talar Roudaki - and a sizeable surplus at that. There was a widespread expectation that it would be the Iranian dancers who were most likely to be first in the firing line. I wondered if Arash might be one of them. Whilst no one questioned his considerable stage-presence or talent for acting out dramatic roles, he struggled with his classical technique, having only begun formal ballet training in his late teens. Fortunately his name was not on any list. Still, rumours and gossip relating to redundancies and sackings spread like wildfire, the atmosphere rapidly souring as suspicion and fear began to grip the Persian dancers. Within a few days a clear schism had emerged and you could divide company members into two distinct camps -the old guard and the new.

The weaker Iranian dancers would look on in awe as the new American recruits performed what seemed like supernatural warm up stretches, contorting their bodies into forced positions - of little interest to those of us who had benefited from Inga and Robert's Russian training. The company's in-house Savak informant, *Behrouz the spy*, as he was known, wasted no time before springing into action, attempting to ingratiate himself with the new Director. Standing close to Ali Gholampour, he did what by now came naturally to him, whispering snippets of information. 'That pretty girl over there with the light hair in the corner is Maggie. She's English and has lived here for many years. Her husband is Jamshid - our lead male dancer'. Seeing Ali Gholampour's eyes focus on me, Behrouz lowered his voice, as if about to reveal something terribly damning, a disclosure so awful it might in due course come to seal my own fate. 'That's Clair. She has been with the company for about five years and is married to Arash.' His eyes narrowing, he then put down what he no doubt considered to be his trump card. 'She's a Jew.'

It soon emerged that the dancers' fears and suspicions were well founded - within a matter of weeks only a few of the Iranian dancers remained in the company. It felt as if there had been a *coup d'état*. Nejad Ahmadzadeh had been given his marching orders. The Russian ballet masters had gone. The tightly knit fabric of the company, carefully crafted by Madame Inga and Monsieur Robert over many years, had similarly disintegrated before my eyes. Now mediocre ballet classes were given by the new director, an American import, in keeping with much of the military hardware which formed the backbone of the Shah's army. Although I had managed to survive the culling of the *corps de ballet* I felt distinctly uneasy with the situation, a sense of injustice and outrage, disloyal to my friends and rapidly came to the conclusion that it was Ali Gholampour who constituted the source of all evil - just as Mr. Ahmadzadeh had done before him. But my hostility towards our new director evidently went unheard or undetected because I was soon being offered soloist roles within the new regime. And if it had been the intention of *Behrouz the spy* to stir up some latent underlying anti-Semitism from deep within the psyche of Ali Gholampour, he was entirely unsuccessful in that regard. Hardly surprising in some respects - he had spent much of his life in New York City -where he had evidently been able to see for himself that Jews were not enemy aliens.

Arash had been looking tired and haggard for some time. But then I noticed a change. His spirits lifted, he held me close to him - a most unusual treat - and looked at me purposefully. 'I am optimistic about the outcome of all those medical tests - I am confident that it won't be long now before I am granted exemption from the army. And exemption means passport.' After four years of plotting and planning his exit strategy from Iran this represented potentially life-changing news.

With the outcome of his ongoing efforts to obtain a passport remaining uncertain, Arash found it difficult to hide his frustrations. But the more tests and obstacles he encountered, the more determined and resolute he seemed to become. One mid-afternoon, as I poured out a tea from a large silver samavar, and set about helping Shahin and Sholeh prepare the evening meal, Arash appeared in the doorway, clutching a piece of paper tightly in his hand. He looked at each of us in the kitchen and then announced emotionally, 'I am the bearer of good news'. Lifting his right hand high in the air he said 'this is my passport to freedom - I am henceforth officially exempted from having to do army service'. It was a rare moment of jubilation. Shahin could not conceal her relief - she had been obliged to stand by helplessly watching her son slip in and out of depression, his sense of imprisonment in Iran almost palpable. Now, at last, he had been given the opportunity of rebuilding his life. 'Look Clair', he said, showing me the precious document. 'This is what I've been working towards. All that time. All those visits. All of those tests. All of that waiting. Now all I have to do is get one final letter which will enable me to collect my passport.' I smiled, hardly able to believe what I had just heard. If all went well, this was more than a mere turning point in our lives - its ripples would be felt not only in Banafsheh Street but at my parents' home in London too. We would finally be able to leave Iran. It would be the beginning of a new life together. If it was Arash's dream to leave Iran, then it was most certainly my dream too.

'And there is something else', he added. 'I also think that the time has come for you to leave the company - if you would be happy to do so, that is.' Happy? I was only too delighted. It was not that I hadn't grown to love Iran, its people, its customs and traditions. I had. The Alizadeh family too - including my father-in-law Parviz - who for

131

reasons he chose never to disclose had once failed to enter an appearance on his son's wedding day. But I knew that Arash's feeling of imprisonment within the borders of Iran went to the heart of his malaise. It had to follow, therefore, that once able to operate under the auspices of a more progressive regime, his depression would quickly come to belong to the past, he would cease to keep me at arm's length from virtually every aspect of his life, his previous charm and good humour would swiftly return and, in common with Candide's mentor Pangloss in Voltaire's biting satire on optimism, I believed with all my heart that once out of Iran Arash would be a different person, reborn in a sense, and that *everything would be for the best in the best of all possible worlds.* That at least was what I longed for - it was the essence of my strategy to reclaim the man I had fallen in love with and continued to love. His passport to freedom would be our passport to renewal and renovation. Immediately I began to imagine my parents' joy at the prospect of my return. Except this time with my husband. I rather wish it had been lyrics drawn from Persian verse or song which came to me. But it was not. Instead the wording of an old Negro spiritual spontaneously danced around my mind. *'Free at last! Free at last!'* And then the refrain would begin, so clearly and effectively that I was left with little option other than to say it out loud. *'Thank God Almighty, we are free at last!'*

Whereupon I came back down to earth with a bump - there were more mundane matters to attend to. How should I go about terminating my contract at Talar Roudaki? What period of notice would be required? Arash advised me not to trouble myself unduly with the niceties of Iranian employment law. 'I wouldn't worry about that kind of thing ', he said adamantly. 'Ali Gholampour has seen to it that most of the original dancers have now lost their jobs. They have no other skills at all. That means that he has thrown them all onto the scrap heap.'

I decided there and then that Ali Gholampour should receive a taste of his own medicine - and that I would be the one to dish it out. I would walk out of the company forthwith. It would be my gesture of defiance, an act of solidarity with the Iranian dancers who had become such an integral part of five extraordinary years spent at Talar Roudaki. But the Iranian National Ballet Company, originally backed by Her Majesty the Shahbanou, had come to languish under an equally imperial but now predominantly American occupying regime and I, for one, wished to have no part of it.

Still, it was a strange sensation for the ballet company to no longer constitute part of my daily routine. Not that my lone protest was dramatic in nature - all that happened was that I failed to show up for work. Nothing was said, no one called. I wondered if they were perhaps happy to be rid of me too. Then, just a few days later, Arash came into our bedroom and handed me an envelope. He had a rather triumphant look on his face, which made me wonder whether it was an urgent request for me to quickly pack my *pointe* shoes and hurry back to Talar Roudaki. Or, better still, perhaps the envelope contained Arash's passport. 'Open it', he said, barely able to suppress a smile. In fact it was neither of my imaginary scenarios. It was an Iran Air ticket - a one way ticket made out in my name, destination UK. 'That's great Arash', I said. 'But there's only one ticket here - where is yours?'

'I haven't been able to buy mine yet, I'm afraid. You know why not - I still haven't received my passport.' I sat with the ticket on my lap, my enthusiasm for the trip rapidly diminishing. 'It's not what I would have wished - but you are going to have to go back on your own.' No special skill was required to see the disappointment in my eyes. 'You always said though that...' but before I could finish my sentence, he added 'nor can I give you an exact date as to when I will be able to leave Tehran.' I held up the ticket which by now had come to represent separation, precisely the opposite of what I had been seeking to obtain. 'Things never go as planned in this country, Clair, especially when it comes to Iranian bureaucracy and officialdom.' He took my hand, told me not to worry, asked me to fly off without him, promised me faithfully that he would follow at the first opportunity and having in effect presented me with a *fait accompli* I was left with little choice other than to agree.

There were no grand farewells at the Alizadeh residence in Banafsheh Street. Why should there have been? Having spent the last five years flying back and forth between Tehran and London, always for the purpose of visiting my parents, this departure resembled any other.

133

I hugged Shahin and Sholeh and said goodbye to the rest of my warm and loving Iranian family.

Arash drove me to the airport and helped me with my heavy suitcase. I held him tightly, unsure of when we would next see one another again. I felt the warmth and security of his arms around my waist. Reluctantly dragging myself away towards the departure lounge I could see the emotion in his eyes. 'See you soon then', I whispered. And with those words I left Iran. Alone.

Chapter 19: From Iranian Chalk to Irish Cheese

I could, I suppose, attempt to package it rather grandly. And write that barely three months later I was hired as a soloist in the Irish National Ballet, based in Cork, the third largest city on the magnificent Emerald Isle. But the truth was that there was nothing at all grand about the Irish National Ballet. It was the autumn of 1977, I was 24 years old, eager for my new contract to get underway, confident in my ballet technique - from a professional point of view this should have been my big break. It was not.

Of course I was flattered to have been engaged as a lead. I had been put through my paces at an audition in London by the company's artistic advisor, the Israeli choreographer Domy Reiter-Soffer. When he offered me the job, I immediately heard Arash's voice encouraging me to turn it down, rebuking me for collaborating with an agent of the *Zionist entity,* a phrase for which he had a preference on the grounds that saying the word Israel out loud somehow conferred legitimacy on the Jewish state. But I concluded that it was ludicrous to make a link between the role Reiter-Soffer had in mind for me, based on the legend of Phaedra in Greek mythology, and the contentious politics of the Middle East. And so, for once, I decided to ignore the unsolicited advice I was attributing to Arash but which continued to be heard in my head.

As with the Iranian National Ballet, the Irish National Ballet was a relatively new company, having been established just four years prior to my arrival in Cork. But there ended any common ground between Ireland and Iran. For as rich and opulent as the Iranian National Ballet was so the Irish National Ballet was strapped for cash and hard-up. It was the brainchild of the former Irish Step Dance champion and war pipes musician turned choreographer Joan Moriarty. She had spent some years locked in battle with the Arts Council of Ireland attempting to persuade those responsible for the allocation of grants to back her new venture. Although eventually successful, the Irish company was nevertheless plagued by chronic underfunding from the outset. In practical terms this meant that when it came to the rehearsal rooms it was immediately apparent that I had not pulled off a particularly good deal, having swapped the extravagance and ostentatiousness of Talar Roudaki for a dark and dingy church hall in Cork. In fact the ballet company had no permanent home of its own as such - even within its host city. Whereas the origin of the name Tehran was unknown I soon found out the word Cork comes from the Irish *Corcaigh* meaning *swamp,* local information which I could have well done without during my first few days in the southwest of Ireland.

Still, I tried to put on a brave face in front of the Irish, English and American dancers preparing for the morning class. The small changing area was a converted kitchen canteen. But the banter was friendly enough amongst company members and morale high as the ballet master waved a casual hello to the assembled group. A large baggy jersey struggled to cover his protruding stomach; straight brown hair left to find a style of its own. I hoped that his classes would be more inspiring than his demeanour. They were not.

Whereas in Tehran I had a caring family to return to, in Cork my living conditions were grim. The only redeeming feature was that I was sharing with a couple who I knew well from the company in Iran - Ros and Amin. They too had been engaged by the Irish National Ballet. In our hurry to find rented accommodation, we made the mistake of taking the first maisonette offered - but number 3 Walsh's Place, Leitrim Street happened to be entirely devoid of any natural daylight in the main living area.

To begin with Amin's Middle Eastern ways and handsome balletic appearance reminded me of what I missed most - Arash. But very soon his behaviour began to change. He became quiet and withdrawn, sloppy in appearance, started to chain smoke and would regularly fail to turn up for work. As he slipped into a pattern of drinking heavily throughout the day, the atmosphere in the house soured, his relationship with Ros strained.

'I'm not sure what to do', Ros confided to me one day whilst shuffling our feet in the resin box just before class. 'You can see how he has changed Clair, can't you? In Tehran Amin used to brighten up the studio with his quick wit and boisterous spirit. But now, especially over these past few months, he has gradually become quiet and withdrawn. As for his drinking, it's awful, I can't see our relationship lasting long if he carries on like this to be honest with you. Good job we're not married, hey?' I felt very sorry for Ros but I was hardly able to give a master-class in how to achieve a satisfactory relationship myself. 'Let's just forget about these men, at least while we are in class' I suggested. I could see how she yearned to have the old Amin back. I could see that because I had the same yearning for Arash, the old Arash, the one I had been charmed by in Tehran during our early, heady days. If I was hoping that work might lift our flagging spirits, I was mistaken. For neither classes nor rehearsals proved to be a source of much inspiration. I had been lured to Cork by the innovative choreography of Domy Reiter-Soffer - only to find that the role of Phaedra was to be learned not from the great man himself but via a few video recordings and an occasional helping hand from company members.

When, finally, I would retire to bed, my dreams would often carry me off into Arash's arms - dreams so real that I could touch his face, smell his skin and lay my head on his shoulder. During those brief interludes I would feel utterly serene and at peace. Only to be woken up by Amin's coughing and spluttering as he set about trying to clear his throat of catarrh and phlegm whilst attempting to get some fresh air into his nicotine polluted lungs. Annoyed at being disturbed from my dreams, I would grudgingly open my eyes and confront my new reality - alone in a small double-bed in a room reeking of damp and mould, with smoke from Amin's first cigarette of the day managing to find its way under my door. The idea of being a soloist in the Irish National Ballet company continued to sound glamorous when presented to others. But the truth was that I was as far from living the dream as one could imagine - nightmare was the word which sprang more readily to mind.

Of course news from Arash would have been a tonic. Any news - even a snippet. But there was nothing. Only silence. My naturally high spirits were being dragged into a downward spiral. I would avoid going back to my digs immediately after work and instead visit the local pub with other company members. Although a Bloody Mary would go down well I knew that upping my intake of alcohol was unlikely to resolve the issues confronting me. I developed a craving for chocolates and cakes - anything sweet which could provide a quick sugar fix - and as a result put on so much weight so rapidly that I began to have difficulty fitting into my clothes. Then, more worryingly, I missed a period. And a second month's too. I booked an appointment with a local GP and rattled off a list of my woes: I was unhappy with my living conditions, frustrated at work, had put on a considerable amount of weight and my menstrual cycle was entirely out of sync. When the doctor pronounced his initial diagnosis, I didn't know whether to laugh or cry. 'I *tink* it could be *de case*', he declared in a delightful Irish lilt, '*dat* you are pregnant. Is it at all possible *dat* you could be in *de* family way?' 'Of course not', I replied, 'I haven't seen my husband for three months - or anyone else for that matter'. I walked out of the surgery with my own, more accurate, diagnosis - I was depressed. Yet how I longed to be carrying Arash's child. But that was something, alas, with which even the legendary luck of the Irish would be unable to assist.

Not for the first time ballet proved to be my salvation. As the pace of rehearsals for Reiter-Soffer's *Chariots of Fire* stepped up a notch in anticipation of the opening season in Cork I managed to learn the role of Phaedra, the undoubted highlight of which was an erotic duet with my stepson Hippolytus, a role played by a talented Mexican-born dancer by the name of Babil Gandara. It was a duet which embodied an extraordinarily dramatic statement of love and jealousy, despair and eventual death. Drawing mainly on the play by Racine, but with more than a passing reference to Euripides too, accompanied by the well-chosen music of three contemporary Greek composers, Reiter-Soffer had choreographed the *pas de deux* in a most provocative and seductive manner, a frenzy of lust and passion, arms and legs intertwined. I wondered what Arash would have made of such an overt display of sexuality.

Having walked the short distance home from church hall rehearsal rooms to shabby maisonette in the fading light of a chilly late November afternoon, I was impatient to shower off and freshen up. Just as I was beginning to unwind and relax, sharing stories of the day's activities with Ros in the tiny kitchenette, the telephone rang.
'It's for you Clair', she said, handing me the receiver. It was always so comforting to hear the sound of my father's voice. After a short

chat about how the ballet *Chariots of Fire* was shaping up - I spared him a detailed account of its explicit choreography - the tone of his voice gave little away. Then he came out with it. 'I have good news for you darling. Arash is out - he has left Iran.' Silence. 'Clair?' 'I'm here dad'. Had I heard him correctly? 'Clair' he repeated. 'Arash is out of Iran, he is on his way to you right now as we speak'. Ros had been edging her way towards me. Having seen the ghostly expression on my face, she must have imagined that I was the unfortunate recipient of some dreadful news. But upon hearing my screams of delight she immediately mouthed the name Arash to me, gave an inquisitive thumbs up sign, to which I responded with an affirmative nod.

Still breathless, I thanked my father for calling. His call - the news I had been waiting for. It had been a long time coming. My husband was now not far away.

Chapter 20: Prince Ali

Of course it didn't take long to tidy my small room. I pleaded with Ros and Amin to keep the maisonette similarly spick and span. I was determined that everything should be right for Arash's arrival in Cork. I was equally determined that nothing would ever keep us apart again. A couple of days went by without any news. That then turned into a couple of weeks - still no word of his whereabouts. After a third week of nagging my housemates to adhere to unusually high standards of orderliness, I was beginning to sound rather tiresome, even to myself. Where on earth was he? Company members began to tease me about the absence of Ali - Arash was apparently far too strange a name for them to grapple with - and would make up an elaborate story about a handsome Persian dancer, a certain Prince Ali, who had mysteriously abandoned his true love, allowing her to languish on a remote corner of the island of Ireland. As the scenarios became increasingly complex and far-fetched, we would end up in tears of laughter. But the truth was that I had begun to wonder if behind such bonhomie there might not be just an element of truth. I ran through the timings - they were hardly difficult to work out. A week to pack his bags and say his farewells, a day's travel for the flight from Tehran to Heathrow, a night or two with my parents in London before the short trip over to Cork. That could surely only run to a maximum of ten days. But now over double that period of time had elapsed and there was still no sign of Arash - Ali - people could call him what they liked, he remained the man I loved.

Finally, almost a month after his initial call, my father phoned again. Arash had boarded an Aer Lingus flight to Cork and was due to arrive later that day. I could hardly believe my eyes when, finally, he came through the smoky sliding glass doors. As we caught sight of one another, I felt a flush of heat wash over my body, my knees wobbling as I observed his kindly eyes light up, his lips breaking into a warm and spontaneous smile. I had to pinch myself to ensure it was all for real - not simply another night of wishful dreaming. Within seconds I had melted into his affectionate embrace, where I would have happily remained had it not been necessary to make our way back to the modest maisonette just a few minutes from the city centre.

Arash's arrival also caused a stir within the ballet company where there were loud welcoming cheers for the eternally elusive Prince Ali. He took it all in good spirit and teased them back with stories of his protracted journey across wild poppy fields, deserts and tumultuous seas to reclaim but one of his many wives who had somehow managed to slip away from the harem to a most strange and distant land where leprechauns, goblins and pixies lived in harmony with the local population. He was soon given permission to take classes with the company as a guest dancer - his charm was working its magic once more.

Almost immediately my life became sweeter, lighter - as if the weight that had been dragging me down had miraculously been removed, its accompanying mist lifting from around my head, enabling me to focus on my role as Phaedra with a new crispness and clarity. I began to feel so good about all things Irish that I developed an agenda of my own: my hope was for Arash to audition for and be accepted as a fully fledged member of the Irish National Ballet. We would work together again - just as we had in Iran.

It seemed appropriate, if somewhat unoriginal, to celebrate our reunion on our first Saturday night together by treating ourselves to a meal at a smart restaurant in the centre of town. Uncorking a bottle of cabernet sauvignon our wine glasses clinked together in unison as we drank to each other's health and a bright new future together outside Iran, the small solitary candle on the table flickering gently as we did so, its soft yellow flame reflecting mischievously warm shadows from Arash's dark eyes. The conversation flowed freely – there was so much to catch up on. 'Arash,' I said, putting my hand on top of his. 'I'm so glad you are safe - I've been terribly worried about you.' He looked at me quizzically. 'Well, you took so long to get here, I was sure that something dreadful had happened to you'.

'Oh, Clair *jaan* I am so sorry,' he said. 'I probably should have mentioned it to you earlier'. I noticed him dabbing the restaurant's starched white linen serviette at his mouth, as if attempting to wipe away an unsavoury disclosure. His gaze shifted to the neighbouring table and then quickly back to me. 'What is it - what is it?' I asked impatiently. 'Well, it's just that I met a couple of Iranian friends in

142

Paris before coming on to Cork. And we thought that it might be rather nice to go skiing together for a week in the French Alps.'

'You're joking, I take it. You're joking - aren't you?' I looked into his eyes and saw that it was no joke at all. I immediately became aware of my heart pounding hard, almost announcing its presence to the outside world, my cheeks burning and quickly becoming red with rage. 'To be honest', he added, 'it wasn't even my idea.'

Silence. But not for long. 'You bastard, Arash.' I tried, unsuccessfully, to keep my voice down. 'You absolute bastard. I can't believe that you would deliberately hurt me like that.'

'Sorry Clair - I didn't think you would be able to come with us because of your work', he mumbled unconvincingly.

'But Arash, your sense of priority, what on earth were you thinking? I longed so much to be with you that my body stopped functioning properly. And all for what?' I asked rhetorically. 'For you to go slaloming down the ski slopes of the Alps with a few friends from Tehran? And this is just the beginning of your 'freedom' from Iran - not a particularly honourable start if you ask me.' Whereupon our romantic reunion in one of Cork's smarter restaurants came to an abrupt and untimely end.

As we walked home through a maze of narrow streets and dark alleyways, sorrowfully and estranged, I noticed endless rows of pretty bay windows, small family grocery stores shuttered down for the night, the distinctly pungent aroma of roasted barley - the tell tale sign of the presence of Guinness - and the milky shadows of a full moon lighting up Cork's wintery sky.

Since we had returned to the maisonette in silence I was half expecting Arash to fully embrace this strategy of not speaking - I had witnessed his dishing out a dose of the silent treatment on more than one occasion in Tehran - and knew very well that he was so terribly proud and stubborn that he had the capacity to stop communicating with those who might have incurred his displeasure for weeks at a time. Maybe it was my turn. Once in bed, I tossed and turned into the small hours of the morning. Then, without any conscious thought on my part, I turned towards my husband, drew myself towards his body, put an arm around his chest and, finally, drifted off to sleep.

The following morning I realised that I had not been sent to Coventry at all. Quite the contrary - he had something to say. 'I can't stay here in Cork, Clair'. His tone was business like and matter-of-fact. He had been based in the south of Ireland for less than a fortnight but his short stay there had apparently not prevented him from being able to make up his mind as to what the future might hold. 'Cork is not for me - there is really nothing for me here.'

'Can't you stay, Arash, just for this year?' I implored, 'I'm sure you'll be accepted in the Company and then we can leave Ireland together when my contract comes to an end'.

'I'm sorry Clair, but I can't', he replied adamantly. 'Shideh has enrolled at the Sorbonne where she is a student of French language and literature whilst Sholeh is studying graphic design. They are living in a small flat in the outskirts of Paris. That is where I would like to go and that is where I feel I should be. Paris is where it's all happening. It's come to be the centre of resistance to the Shah's regime you know.'

Although I remained thoroughly disenchanted with Arash's lack of consideration towards me, the very thought of living apart from him again was too much to bear. The following day I handed in my notice - three months were required. I was alone again in Ireland, albeit with a promise that Arash would return to watch me dance the role of Phaedra in the final performance of the season. Although fellow company members understood my need to be with my husband, Aloys Fleischman certainly did not. He had earlier established the Cork Symphony Orchestra and worked alongside Joan Moriarty in setting up not just the Irish National Ballet but the Cork Ballet Company which had preceded it. Fleischman was a hugely influential person in the world of Irish arts - someone you crossed at your peril. I was summonsed to his office where I could see from his frosty reception that I was going to be in for a rough ride. 'I hope you are not thinking of leaving us, Clair, after the Cork season', he said icily, his eyes magnified by thick glasses but all the time staring unblinkingly into my face.   I was taken aback.   There was no secret about my departure, I was working out my notice with a view to rejoining my husband in Paris - I had even consulted an Equity representative who confirmed that I was perfectly within my rights.   He continued unabashed.   'If you do leave us', he said menacingly, 'you will be in breach of the terms of your contract and I shall personally see to it that you are blacklisted.   You understand what that means, don't you? That you will never be able to work in any ballet company again'.   I stood slightly back staring at him - not only one of Ireland's most eminent composers and musicologists but a former Professor of Music at University College Cork.   His face was small and clean shaven, his mouth surly, his eyes dull.   'I suggest you go away and have a little think about it', he continued quietly, 'you might find that you want to review your position'.   But my mind was already made up.   No threat implied or real, was capable of keeping me away from Arash - I was already counting the days before I would see him again.

This time Arash was true to his word.   He returned from Paris to watch me dance the role of the tormented seductress Phaedra in *Chariots of Fire*.   The Irish Times' art critic Seamus Kelly had already written a rave review, praising Reiter-Soffer's interpretation of the blood-soaked Greek tragedy, his only regret the absence of *'enough superlatives to describe this major work of great choreographical feats and exciting scenes'*.   As the ballet moved towards its inevitable climax I danced in perfect harmony with my stepson Hippolytus, our arms and hands moving as one, our bodies intertwined in a frenzied display of passion and lust, the audience bursting into spontaneous applause as the final curtain came down. Apart from one particular spectator sitting in the stalls of Cork's historic Opera House and whose eye I happened to catch.   It was Arash.   He was not at all impressed by the sexually explicit nature of our *pas de deux* and afterwards made little reference to the ballet I had spent the previous months preparing for, with all of the highs and lows it had entailed.

The following day I set off with Arash for France.   With my confidence rock-solid that it would be within the confines of the

French capital - the world's most romantic city - that I would at long last be able to reclaim my husband.

Chapter 21: Plus ça Change

It was during these first few months of 1978, when my own professional preoccupations were related to the interpretation of the role of Phaedra, that the first fatal casualties were suffered in major demonstrations against the Shah. In the city of Najaf, in Iraq, the son of Ayatollah Khomeini had been found dead in his bed. Precisely what killed him was destined to remain a mystery, partly because autopsies are not allowed in Islam. But Arash was convinced that the finger of suspicion pointed towards Savak, the Shah's much feared security services, an acronym synonymous with the brutality and repression of the Peacock throne. Of course during my five years in Iran I had come to understand that the Shah was not terribly receptive to the notion of opposition in general and to his regime in particular. So when theological colleges in Iran's holy city of Qom closed down in protest at what they considered to be the deliberate slaying of Mustafa Khomeini, the Ayatollah's son, a sizeable contingent of police officers was dispatched to quell the unrest. Arash had written to me that within moments of their arrival guns had been aimed at the demonstrators. Seminary students, with a mixture of youthful bravado and religious fervour had actually dared his Imperial Majesty's officers to shoot. Scores of demonstrators were killed on the spot. Whereupon the Ayatollah Khomeini - the future Supreme Leader of Iran - although still in exile in Iraq, immediately called for further demonstrations not just in Iran but around the world. The Iranian embassy in Paris came under attack by Iranian students and local communist youth groups. 'Politically things are changing by the minute', Arash said. 'Now there are even rumours that Saddam Hussein, the Vice President of Iraq, is so fed up with the presence of the Ayatollah in his country that he might shortly be exiled again'. In fact that was no rumour at all. It was true, the Ayatollah's eyes apparently set on a quiet but historic village just 40 kilometres to the west of the *Champs-Élysées*. It was into this febrile atmosphere of pre-revolutionary Iranian politics that I had arrived with Arash. It was as if Tehran had come to the French capital. I realised right away what this meant - and it did not augur well.

I'm not attempting to suggest that I was in any sense some sort of simple soul, disinterested in the major issues of the day. Not at all.

147

But at the same time it still struck me as slightly bizarre that my entire life had come to be inextricably bound up with issues of international politics over which I, an unemployed ballet dancer in Paris, had not the slightest influence or control. Not that my living conditions in Paris were the hub of dissent or opposition to the Shah's regime - I was based in the tiny studio apartment which Arash had been sharing with his sisters Shideh and Sholeh, all expenses for which were being picked up by their father Parviz. Situated on the ground floor of a sizeable grey stone building near the Château de Vincennes, the area was connected to the capital on the city's cheap and efficient métro. The high ceilinged living space was multi-purpose-bedroom, dining room and lounge. Although delighted to meet up with my Iranian family again I could see that a single room for the four of us was likely to be a tough call. As bedtime approached we would set about folding away the collapsible table and put it to one side - the freed up area immediately occupied by a double mattress earmarked for Arash and me. But with space at a premium it invariably ended up nudging against the sofa-bed upon which my sisters-in-law slept.

Of course this was hardly the ideal environment in which the sexual side of our relationship might flourish, although my attraction to Arash had not diminished. And so I would find myself drawn to his side, eager to feel the touch of his hands, impatient for the process of seduction to begin. I soon came to realise that I would be likely to continue waiting for some time on the grounds that out of the four people lying there I happened to be the only one who remained awake. Reluctantly abandoning any hopes of intimacy, I would snuggle up closely to Arash and join him in sleep.

It was as well that there was the elegance and grace of Paris all around. I would picnic with Shideh and Sholeh in the nearby *Bois de Vincennes*, sprawling parkland originally frequented by the Kings of France who had once used it as their hunting reserve. While my sisters-in-law attended lectures and tutorials at the Sorbonne, I would head off to ballet classes to ensure that I remained in shape. And then it happened, shortly after dinner and as the dishes were being cleared away, that unwelcome but all too familiar refrain. Arash popped his head around the kitchen door. 'See you later then', he said to the three of us busily clearing up in the tiny kitchenette. I

148

immediately felt heaviness in my chest - a sensation last experienced whilst in Tehran - because I knew precisely what was coming next.

'Where are you off to?' I enquired. 'I have to go out Clair, there is a lot of political activity in downtown Paris and I want to be part of it.' I could tell by the expression on his face that it was pointless even to ask if I might accompany him. But I tried nevertheless. I could have written the wording of his reply because I had heard various formulations of it on so many occasions in Iran. 'I have to go alone Clair. I'm meeting up with a few Iranian friends - you would end up sitting alone listening to us discussing politics in Farsi all night long. You really are better off here with Sholeh and Shideh'. And that, it seemed, was my destiny. To be abandoned again by my husband - except this time in a small studio apartment in the outskirts of the French capital.

On 21st March 1978 - a few weeks before my 25th birthday - I received an unexpected letter from my father. Since he wrote rarely I was impatient to read its contents. Still, I decided to save it for my journey on the métro on the way in to class. It contained a round-up of all the family's news, precisely as I had expected. After a while though my father moved to the heart of the matter - what it was he really wanted to say.

I am having some difficulty in understanding what you are up to in Paris. It seems to me as if you are wasting your time there, in conditions which, if I have understood them correctly, are far from satisfactory at all. What are your future plans for auditioning for another ballet company - do you have any? My main concern, though, relates to you and Arash. He isn't providing for you at all, my darling, he isn't working and I would be less than honest were I not to tell you that this weighs on my mind very heavily indeed. Your mother and I are both worried for you. Darling, I would like you just to think about this -don't reply right away - just think about it, please, for me. Is Arash really the right husband for you? Would you not, perhaps, be better off without him? I don't need to tell you that you are always in my thoughts and I shall close this letter by sending you lots of kisses and my fondest love - Dad.

I could feel the weight of my father's concern in every written word. In fact I could hear his voice so clearly it was as if he were sitting there right next to me, whispering his confidential counsel. As the carriage sped through the stops of Reuilly-Diderot and Bastille, en route to town, I struggled with my conscience. My father was of the old school where emotions were rarely allowed to see the light of day. I knew that it must have been difficult for him to put pen to paper. And of course much of what he said was true. Yet I had become accustomed to living communally with Arash's family whilst in Iran - in that respect nothing had changed. I shook my head gently, as if to free myself from any negative feelings towards Arash. I left the *métro* at Palais Royal-Musée du Louvre, dance bag slung over shoulder, my emotions raw and exposed. As I climbed the staircase and headed towards the Rue de Rivoli, the stylish street Napoleon Bonaparte had built through the centre of Paris, I tore my father's heart-felt missive into several pieces, placing the shredded bundle into the first rubbish bin I could find. Nothing could be allowed to undermine my marriage.

My spirits were nevertheless lifted during the following few weeks with the arrival of warmer weather and the delights of Paris in the spring. Then a rather pleasant surprise came my way. Shideh and Sholeh had taken a last minute decision to return to Tehran for the two week Easter break from the Sorbonne. They had purchased their tickets, packed their bags and were ready to leave on an Iran Air flight the following day. That might not sound like earth-shattering news - but it was to me. It would be the first opportunity for Arash and I to live as a couple - just the two of us - the first time in five years of marriage. I could hardly believe my luck - it felt as if a most magnificent gift from the Gods had been bestowed upon me. I began to imagine it as a belated honeymoon, walking hand in hand with Arash along the banks of the Seine, dining in inexpensive restaurants, romantic boat rides in the city's *bateaux mouches* - perhaps even a visit to the Paris ballet. But even doing nothing at all would be a real treat - we would still be together, *à deux*. Just a few of those precious days had passed when the telephone rang. It was Arash's mother Shahin calling from Iran. After an exchange of the usual courtesies and having enquired after everyone's health, I handed the receiver to Arash. As he chatted away in rapid fire Farsi I soon noticed a change in tone. His face became concerned, his voice apprehensive and unsure, he appeared to be nodding in earnest agreement with whatever his mother was saying at the other end of the line.

'What is it?' I enquired. But he was so involved in his own thoughts he looked right through me.

'Arash', I said, with a little more urgency. 'Has something happened? Is everyone alright? It soon emerged that everything was not alright. One of Arash's friends from Tehran was unwell. I hardly knew Saranjam Husani, the name he mentioned, not least because I had always been kept at arm's length from his closest confidants in Iran. He had become unwell whilst working in the southern port city of Bandar Abbas on the Persian Gulf, some 1500 kilometres to the south of the Iranian capital. He had struggled to adjust to the exceptionally high humidity and heat there. Hardly surprising - temperatures can soar towards 50 degrees. It was whilst suffering in such searing heat that he had picked up a dangerous disease transmitted by the tsetse fly. The doctors referred to it as human African trypanosomiasis although everyone else called it sleeping sickness. 'He's in a bad way Clair,' Arash explained. 'My mother has asked me to take care of him - he needs urgent medical treatment in Paris. If it's not tackled properly it can apparently be fatal.'

I felt guilty for being more concerned with what I considered to be thoroughly poor timing than the well-being of Arash's friend. But I was soon able to put matters into perspective and set about tidying the apartment, making up the sofa-bed and preparing for his arrival. It was during this intervening period that I noticed Arash's thoughts were elsewhere. Eventually I enquired what was troubling him.

'Well you know that Saranjam is on his way, don't you?' 'Of course I do', I said light-heartedly, 'I've just prepared the sheets and bed for him.' 'Well, that's the point. I am not a devout Muslim, as you know, but you must surely also be able to see that it would not be right for you to share a room with two men'. I could see where this was going and I didn't like it at all. 'Okay then', I said, 'why don't we find a nearby hotel or a homely chambre d'hôte for Saranjam?' 'But he's sick, Clair, and you know very well that he doesn't speak a word of French.'

'So,' I said, with rising anger, 'what exactly do you have in mind?'

He looked right at me. 'I would like you to leave.'

'But Arash, what are you talking about? I am your wife'. I felt my hands beginning to tremble.

'Listen to me. It wouldn't be for long and you could visit your parents. It's just not right for you to be here with the two of us in the flat. It's as simple as that.'

A few days later, suitcase in hand, I knocked on the front door of my parents' home. They had moved from Regents Park and were now living in an attractive detached bungalow in Loughton, part of the Epping Forest area of Essex. Arash was right - they were indeed delighted to see me. I explained to them what had happened - the circumstances surrounding the arrival of Saranjam and his sleeping sickness.

'I just can't understand how you allowed Arash to do this to you', my father exclaimed. He was mortified. 'Why, why on earth do you allow yourself to be treated in this way?'

I replied in the only way I knew - from the heart.

'Because I love him daddy. Because I love him.'

Chapter 22: A Black Tie Affair

If my move from the Iranian National Ballet company in Tehran to that of the Irish in Cork had represented a rather rapid descent down the artistic pecking order, then in career terms the transition from attending professional classes in Paris to teaching keep fit in various church halls and other addresses in Essex must surely have constituted hitting rock bottom.   I had been given my marching orders from the studio apartment in Paris by my husband in order to make way for his friend and had no immediate intention of auditioning for another ballet company on the grounds that I did not know what Arash's plans might be or how long my exile from Paris might endure. And although I loved my parents dearly, being made to feel welcome at all times, I was only too well aware that my situation was as unsatisfactory as it was unconventional - a 25 year old married woman living with her parents, away from her husband and with no immediate prospects of his return in sight.   Which was why I soon set about devising a strategy to turn matters back to my advantage.   It was a difficult environment in which to think clearly.   At home, my parents' home, I should say, it was easy to see that my father was not well disposed towards his absent son-in-law, his temper becoming unusually quick, his mood uncharacteristically grave.   My role, it seemed, was constantly to seek to excuse the inexcusable.   Not just to family and friends but to myself as well.   As I cast my mind back to the ballet company in Iran and the many months in both Ireland and France, I wondered if the situations in these countries shared a common theme, were linked by a unifying thread.   And then it struck me.   Could it be the case that Arash had never really considered me to be his lawfully wedded wife?   For the simple reason that right from the outset our marriage had been nothing more than an elaborate ploy concocted by my father, its primary purpose the retention of my British passport.   It had never been registered with the relevant authorities in Iran. Why should it have been?   Although we had scrupulously followed specific criteria laid down in the Koran, in practical terms it had been nothing more than a religious ceremony followed by a party at home -Arash's parents' home, that is.   When it came to the issue of wedlock and matrimony, I thought, there was in reality no sound legal footing - in Iranian law, in English law or legislation pertaining to any other jurisdiction for that matter.

Perhaps the truth was that I didn't have a husband at all. There was only one aspect about which I could be completely sure - that there was an absence of any home which I could call my own - nor was there even the remotest sign of Arash being involved in an ongoing battle to provide one.

Almost five months after my departure from Paris, Arash came to visit me in London. During this time I did my best to sustain myself on a diet to which I had reluctantly grown accustomed: the occasional phone call and affectionate but all too infrequent hand-written letters. And I learned right away that Arash's visit was only for an extended weekend. Whilst Saranjam was making progress in his battle against sleeping sickness, his recovery remained far from complete. Of course I was delighted to see Arash after such a prolonged period apart. But my father was not - and this immediately cast a shadow over his stay. It soon emerged that a key element of Arash's trip was to stock up on supplies of babywear. Not with a view to my falling pregnant, alas, but for his cousins, family and friends all of whom apparently appreciated English rather than Iranian baby ware. Arash's task was to dispatch or deliver them as and when he could. It was while accompanying him on the first of what would turn out to be several shopping expeditions to the main Mothercare store in London's West End that I decided to say what was on my mind. Clinging to a large blue and white plastic bag bulging with baby clothes, I said 'I would have loved these to have been for our baby'. He looked at me preoccupied. 'Yes, really', I insisted, 'I would.' But first I would like us to get married again'. Before he had a chance to respond I added, 'except this time under English law'. He immediately laughed out loud. But realising that I was deadly serious, he stopped in his tracks, perplexed. 'But Clair *jaan*, we are already married. It might not be recognised by English law but as far as I'm concerned the vows I took in Tehran in front of your parents and my mother are as sacred to me as any.' I wasn't going to be distracted by talk of solemn pledges and sacred vows - that was all a lot of hot air - for the truth of the matter was that we had hardly ever been together as man and wife at all.

'Well', he said acknowledging the strength of my feelings, 'I don't suppose there is any harm in it, but let's not rush into another marriage ceremony, at least not for the time being.' I completed the shopping with my spirits lifted. Arash picked up on the change in my mood and held my hand tightly before using his humour to good effect. 'Clair *jaan*', he said, 'you know, some day I'm going to find you a *good* husband.' I punched him gently on the arm as we walked off hand in hand to catch the tube at Marble Arch. Two days later he returned to Paris, alone.

I would never have dared say so to my parents but I could understand why Arash continued to be drawn to the French capital. It was at this time - the October of 1978 - that Ayatollah Khomeini was deported from Iraq. He had initially headed for Kuwait - only to be refused entry. Undeterred, he made his way to France where he did not seek political asylum, instead choosing to enter on a tourist visa and settling in the suburb of Neauphle-le-Château. Arash had not witnessed his arrival but he informed me in a letter that it was not difficult to see the hand of the Shah of Iran at work. 'Clair, I have waited for this moment for so long. His regime is now teetering on the brink. But the key thing now is to ensure that any new government will be truly representative of the people and democratic in nature. You can't just overthrow a regime without knowing precisely what will follow.' What Arash was reporting was true - demonstrations involving hundreds of thousands of people had become the order of the day. The Shah had clearly thought that the further the Ayatollah was from Iran, the less trouble he would be, a judgement which would soon prove to be ill-founded on the grounds that telephone connections with Iran and access to the international press were far better than in Iraq. Whatever the case, Paris and its environs had come to be synonymous with opposition to the Shah's regime and although it continued to pain me to be separated from Arash, a part of me was still able to identify with his need to be close to the hub of political change.

My father, however, was not. Not at all. He had come to dislike Arash intensely - his view had remained consistent even if it was not what I wanted to hear - that I was wasting away my best years in a marriage that appeared to be staggering from one crisis to the next. And when he saw me hurting in the process - no matter how hard I tried it was always difficult to hide my emotions from him - then it was hardly surprising that the atmosphere between the two of them should have soured.   But it was Arash's lack of work ethic which grated with my father most of all.   In this respect he shared common ground with Parviz - Arash's own father.   For he too battled to comprehend how his eldest son had failed to embark upon a proper career and was appalled at the absence of any real interest or urgency when it came to the issue of earning a living in his own right.   My father was the opposite of work-shy: upon leaving South Africa for England he had managed to secure employment as an insurance assessor with Sun Alliance - despite coming up for retirement age himself.   Diligent and thorough in the execution of his duties, up and out early every day, it was simply beyond his comprehension to witness Arash's cavalier attitude towards seeking employment.   It would infuriate him to leave Arash, during his occasional visits to London, sitting at the breakfast table engrossed in reading the Daily Telegraph's international affairs section whilst he was setting off to pack in a ten hour day.   Exasperated at Arash's inertia and lack of drive, my father got on the phone himself.   Within a few days he had managed to obtain an interview for him - an administrative position with RIBA, the Royal Institute of British Architects.   Imagine my delight when Arash reported that the meeting had gone well and that he had been offered a job.   Imagine my father's fury when his son-in-law reported to us all that he had turned it down.   'I know this will be disappointing for you to hear but I am sorry, I see my future as part of the new Iran.'

In fact the new Iran was now not far away.   Strikes had been paralyzing the country.   In early December it was estimated that between 6 to 9 million people -more than 10% of Iran's population - marched against the Shah in towns and cities up and down the land. Rioting was widespread.   In a desperate attempt to cling to power he vowed that he would address concerns about the excesses of Savak and promised free and fair elections for the following June.   But it was all too little, too late.   On 16th January 1979, the Shah and his wife the Empress Farah left Tehran and flew to Aswan in Egypt.   The couple's three youngest children were dispatched to the United States. Official reports initially stated that the Shah had left for a holiday and medical treatment.   But the truth was that he had been asked to leave by Shapour Bakhtiar, the man he had appointed prime minister less than two weeks earlier in a last ditch attempt to convince his opponents that he was at long last ready to embrace change.   As news of the Shah's departure spread, there was widespread rejoicing up and down the land - celebrations combined with spontaneous attacks on statues of the Pahlavis.   Within hours almost every visible sign of his dynasty had been destroyed.   So much for *the eternal covenant of the Pahlavi Dynasty with my nation* - the Shah of Iran, Mohammad Rezā Shāh Pahlavi, *Shahanshah* or King of Kings, *Aryamehr* or Light of the Aryans - had finally been ousted.

The Ayatollah Khomeini had always stated that he would not return to Iran until the Shah had left.   In the event he did not have to wait long to remain true to his word.   For fifteen days later, on 1st February 1979, he boarded an Air France flight back to Tehran, his triumphant return just a few hours away.   It was on that flight that the spiritual leader was asked by a prominent American journalist what he felt about the prospect of finally returning to Iran after his long years of exile.   *'Hichi'*, Khomeni replied, 'nothing' - a statement considered reflective of his mystical belief that it was *dar al-Islam* - the area of the world under the rule of Islam - rather than the motherland itself that mattered most.   Those Iranians who might have been hoping for a more mainstream nationalist leader realised right away that they were in for a rude awakening.   Still, as the Ayatollah stepped off of the plane over one million souls were there waiting to greet him.

One would have thought that Arash, a long-standing opponent of the Shah's regime, would have been out there celebrating with them.   He was not.   First of all because the Revolution had happened at a time when he was in London - it was another of his occasional weekends - and secondly because although he was certainly delighted to see the Shah sent packing, he had always argued that it was absolutely crucial to have very precise notions of what you were hoping to achieve and the direction in which you intended to go before even contemplating the replacement of the *ançien regime.*   If Iran was to become an Islamic Republic, would it be tolerant and democratic in nature, would it ensure that the rule of law prevailed, would it respect human rights and ensure that all voices, including those on the left, would be given a fair hearing?   Such a scenario seemed distinctly unlikely.

A few months later, on Friday 18th May, an equally unlikely scenario was scheduled to take place. Arash and I were to be married in a civil ceremony at the Register Office of the Epping Forest district of Essex County Council. Hardly the most glamorous of settings - but it would at least have the benefit of removing any element of ambiguity about the legitimacy of our marriage. It would herald a fresh start for us both and wipe the slate clean in terms of all the pain and anguish that had gone before. It was, in short, the day I had been dreaming of when I would again marry the man I loved.

My mother had catered for a small gathering of family and friends later in the afternoon whilst my father went out of his way to conceal his real feelings and ensure that he would not be seen to be putting a dampener on his daughter's big day. With only a few minutes to go before setting off for Epping town hall Arash looked at me and asked my opinion of his suit. It wasn't often that we both had the occasion to dress so formally and at first glance he looked stunning.

Then I noticed the black tie he had carefully knotted around his neck. I looked at him curiously.

'Arash, black ties are for funerals, you don't want to be wearing that today.' I could see from his expression that he had planned it as a wedding day stunt, a mischievous little joke. But I, for one, was not laughing.

'Clair, I was only joking.' 'Really', he continued, 'this entire process is a joke. I don't understand why you are making us go through this farcical civil ceremony at all'. I could feel my mouth going dry. Although I had explained my reasoning time and again it was clearly not an appropriate moment to reopen the subject. 'If you think that I'm going to be any different by marrying you here today, you are wrong. I'm not going to change - this is how I am - whether it is in Iran, Ireland, France or England. Nothing will make any difference to how I behave. I will never change - this is how I am.'

I stood listening to his tirade, unsure how to react with our departure imminent. 'I do love you Clair', he continued, having removed the offending item, 'but honestly I consider myself married already. I don't need an official piece of paper to tell me what my legal status is.' There was not the time to digest the words he had so casually dished out. But I felt the heavy weight of panic seizing my stomach. A monumental mistake was about to be acted out. But when the time came for us all to set off, I did what I had by now become rather proficient at - closing my ears and eyes to the truth.

The short ceremony was carried out efficiently enough, though cold and soulless in nature. Still, my spirits were stirred somewhat when I heard the kindly Registrar repeat the time-honoured phrase '*I now pronounce you man and wife*' and I officially metamorphosed into Mrs. Clair Alizadeh. My mother had baked a two-tiered chocolate cake for the celebrations later that day and which Arash and I sliced together to enthusiastic applause. As the champagne flowed freely, I spotted my father sitting alone on one of the settees, clutching the long stem of his fluted glass of champagne. With sadness in his eyes, hollowed cheeks and a distinctly pale complexion, he didn't look at all well and I wondered if he had perhaps had a little too much to drink.

Barely three weeks after these rather fraught ceremonials Arash informed me that he would be returning to Tehran. He felt he would be able to make a positive contribution to the evolving political situation in Iran. Precisely what that role was likely to be I did not know for the very good reason that he continued to exclude me from his political manoeuvrings. But the truth was, I suspect, that he did not really know himself, at least not with any precision, the atmosphere in Iran being one of pre-revolutionary turmoil, as political parties and movements, some desperate for democracy, others anxious to establish an Islamic Republic, nervously peered out towards the new but extremely treacherous political landscape.

'Clair, this is the moment for which I have been waiting all my life. I feel that I will be more useful in Iran - especially to those whose voices were never heard by the Shah. The problem is that it's not at all safe for you to accompany me. But as soon as it is I shall call you. This, Clair, is my destiny.'

Mine, it seemed, was to wait for him elsewhere. Alone. Again.

Chapter 23: Khomeini for King

Upon returning to Tehran Arash at least had the good sense to avoid Talar Roudaki. Which was something of a contrast to the approach taken by Avak Abrahamian. Avak was an Armenian, an Armenian Christian, who unlike many dancers in the Iranian National Ballet had managed to survive the sweeping changes introduced by its Iranian-born but American-obsessed new director Ali Gholampour. To begin with he was distinctly upbeat about the prospects of a successful outcome to the recent Revolution in Iran. His view was that because France had come to be the hub of external opposition to the Shah's regime, the Iranian Revolution would come to mirror France's famous Revolution of 1789, when the principles of liberty, equality and fraternity came to be enshrined in the law of the land. He thought that because the French Declaration of the Rights of Man had been so heavily influenced by the Enlightenment, the arts in particular were bound to flourish and would be viewed sympathetically by the new powers that be in Tehran. And therefore that his own future within the ranks of the ballet company was both rosy and secure.

In fact Avak's analysis of the political situation would prove to be so wide of the mark that it can only be described as bordering on the delusional. Or temporarily delusional because within a few weeks of the Ayatollah Khomeini's return, he had not only changed his tune but was even warning fellow company members of what might lie in store. Certainly when he met up with Jeremy Allen, an English ballet dancer and fellow company member, he did not mince his words.
'Jeremy, you must get out of here - never come back to Talar Roudaki. There is a list. The mujahedeen have got a list of names. Of people they are going to kill. Ali Gholampour's name is on it. I don't know about your's - but anyone who had anything to do with the promotion of western culture is in great danger. My own situation is extremely perilous and I am doing my best to get out of here - take my advice, Jeremy, and do the same.'

Easier said than done, the borders of Iran were already closed. Not that that troubled Ali Gholampour unduly - he had had the good sense to set off for New York a few weeks prior to the Revolution and, needless to say, had not the slightest intention of setting foot in the country of his birth for a good many years. Whatever the case, it was clear that the return of Ayatollah Khomeini to Iran was triggering the most tumultuous changes ever seen in the country's history. Not because of the introduction of harsh, repressive measures - the Persian people had long become accustomed to that - but because he was poised to transform Iran into a theocratic Republic. He was well placed to oversee such a transition, being himself perceived as a semi-divine figure, some of those in the enthusiastic crowds chanting *Islam, Islam, Khomeini, We Will Follow You* on the day of his return to Tehran, whilst others bellowed out *Khomeini for King.* The government of Shapour Bakhtiar, appointed during the dying days of the Shah's regime, was given short shrift. '*I shall kick your teeth in*', Khomeini told them. And he did. '*I appoint the government. It is God's government and disobedience is a revolt against God.*' If such notions sound a little unlikely or far-fetched, they were nevertheless well-received by the Iranian people. Within two months of his return a referendum had been held, the question whether or not to replace the monarchy with an Islamic Republic. 98% voted in favour. The introduction of Sharia law was equally swift, Islamic dress code soon being enforced for men and women alike by Revolutionary Guards and other radical groups. Despite the prevailing atmosphere of fear and intimidation at Talar Roudaki, there had been some early attempts by company members for ballet performances to continue - an impossible task when the practice of men and women dancing together was prohibited by decree. That was the final nail in the coffin for the Iranian National Ballet. The broadcasting of any music other than martial or religious was similarly banned. That in turn spelled the end of the Iranian National Orchestra and Opera - the two other institutions with which the ballet company had shared premises at Talar Roudaki. In fact Talar Roudaki itself ceased to exist as Iran's premier venue for the performing arts - it would in due course become a centre for Islamic gatherings.

It was not often that my husband and father found common cause. Arash's last words to me had been that Iran was no longer an environment in which my safety could be assured, an assertion with which my father whole heartedly agreed. Yet neither of them knew precisely why it might be unsafe for me to return to Tehran. In fact it was not related to my being a former member of the Iranian National

Ballet - an inappropriate emblem of a corrupt and immoral culture according to the new regime or that I was a woman, even a western woman for that matter. Nor did it have anything to do with the fact that those opposed to the Ayatollah's Islamic Republic were walking on extremely dangerous ground, for extra-judicial executions soon became widespread. It was, however, everything to do with another potentially lethal combination - my Jewishness and the Ayatollah Khomeini's profound and long-standing anti-Semitism. This was, of course, to be distinguished from his hard-line anti-Israel stance. In some respects I could understand his repudiation of Zionism, if only as a counter-reaction to the former regime's warm embrace of Israel. Although the Shah could never quite bring himself to formally recognise the state of Israel, the two countries had maintained cordial relations, Israel having a permanent delegation in Tehran and which doubled up as a de facto unofficial embassy. No, I am talking here about an old-fashioned form of traditional but virulent anti-Semitism.

The Ayatollah Khomeini had long been aware of the mobilizing power of anti-Semitic rhetoric informing his supporters, back in the 1960s, '*I know you do not want Iran to lie under the boots of the Jews*'. But his broader analysis of the role played by Jews could have been lifted directly from The Protocols of the Elders of Zion - that fictitious and fraudulent text which has the dubious honour of being the most widely distributed anti-Semitic publication of modern times. '*The Jews wish to establish Jewish domination throughout the world. Since they are a cunning and resourceful group of people, they have grasped the world with both hands and are devouring it with an insatiable appetite.*' Anti-semitic rhetoric and writings whilst in exile were one thing, those same sentiments expressed when in power surely quite another. No wonder a chill went down the collective spine of Iranian Jewry when, in August 1979, the Ayatollah spoke of the Banu Qurayza Jews - a cultured and progressive historic tribe from northern Arabia beheaded en masse after being attacked by Mohammad and his army. '*Those who are trying to bring corruption and destruction to our country in the name of democracy will be oppressed. They are worse than the Banu Qurayza Jews and they must be hanged. We will oppress them by God's order and God's call to prayer.*'

There could be little doubt, then, that both Arash and my father were right - I was better off sitting it out during the first few months of the Iranian Revolution with my parents at their home. I would have to wait. I had become accustomed to waiting. But experience in that domain did not mean that it somehow made the process any easier. On the contrary, playing the waiting game became increasingly exasperating, especially with no end in sight. When would it be safe for me to join Arash in Tehran? No one knew. If my husband had the answer, then he made a good job of keeping it to himself, not least because communications with him were few and far between. Every now and then a letter would find its way to Loughton. And once in a while there would be a brief phone call from Tehran. I picked up on the life I had been leading prior to our second marriage ceremony - a combination of assisting my mother in her dance studio and teaching keep-fit in my own right. When people enquired as to the whereabouts of my husband I would always attempt to come up with a positive spin. 'Oh, Arash is in Iran. He feels that he can contribute most to the Revolution by being there.'

Jeremy Josephs had asked me this very question. A law student three years my junior, our paths had crossed through family connections, our first meeting at a dinner party which happened to coincide with one of Arash's occasional visits to London prior to his return to Tehran. He was in a relationship with Vereena Jones, a fellow law student from the University of Leeds. When Arash and I saw Jeremy for the first time we looked at one another knowing perfectly well what the other was thinking - his olive skin and dark features gave him a distinctly Iranian air. He would later disabuse me of that notion, being Essex born and bred. A few months later we met up again.

'Where is your husband?' Jeremy immediately enquired. And I would trot out what had come to sound ominously like the official party line - that he remained in Tehran, that it was still not safe for me to travel out there, that I was waiting for his call.

'I am not trying to put my nose into your private life', he replied, 'but I'm pretty sure you said exactly the same thing six months ago.'

I cannot say with any certainty that there was a direct relationship between the stress my father was undoubtedly experiencing because of the unsatisfactory situation in which I found myself and the subsequent deterioration in his health. Such matters are notoriously difficult to prove. All I could do was observe the symptoms. No medical training was required to know that they were very worrying indeed - a pallid complexion, absence of appetite, loss of weight and despite a significant reduction in the amount of food being consumed a sizable swelling in my father's stomach. Our family doctor immediately referred him to St. Margaret's Hospital in Epping for comprehensive tests. It was agreed that my mother would accompany him on the day.

Upon completion of a most thorough medical examination, but whilst my father was still getting dressed, a nurse informed my mother that the doctor would like to have a word.

'I am very happy to inform you', he announced, 'that there is nothing whatsoever wrong with Mr. Symonds.'

'Well I am very sorry to inform you', my mother replied, 'that I do not accept your diagnosis for one minute. My husband is ill. You can say whatever you like - but I am telling you that my husband is a sick man.'

'Just a minute', the doctor replied. And he rushed off to consult with a more senior person in the hospital hierarchy.

Half an hour later a consultant arrived and introduced himself to my mother.

'I believe you don't accept my colleague's diagnosis', he said, the tone of haughty disapproval only too apparent.

'That's right. I don't. I told the younger doctor who was here a short while ago that my husband is a sick man and he needs your help. Not to be told that he is fine and to go home.'

The consultant was clearly not used to a dose of South African style straight talking or handling forthright characters such as my mother. He appeared slightly shell-shocked by her verbal onslaught.

'Listen', he said, 'its coming up for the Christmas holidays now. Everything is going to go quiet for a while during the Festive Season. What I suggest you do is come back again in the New Year and we will conduct further tests. Meanwhile, I hope that both you and your husband will have a happy and relaxing Christmas.'

My mother had won the showdown, even if there remained a question mark over her husband's health.

'Thank you. And a Merry Christmas to you too.'

Whereupon my father joined me in playing the waiting game.

Chapter 24: Letters to Tehran

The early 1980s might not seem like long ago. But by today's standards that period of time comes across as being back in the dark ages - at least when it comes to methods of communication. With the advent of the internet and smart phones everything now seems instantaneous, immediacy the order of the day. Not so during my sojourns in Ireland and Iran. There were telephones, true enough, but long-distance international calls were prohibitively expensive - if you wanted to speak you soon learned to be brief and to the point. So when it came to attempting to keep open lines of communication with Arash, I came to rely upon a technique which now seems to belong to a positively bygone age - letter writing - and airmail letters at that.

Whilst the Anglo-American broadcaster Alistair Cooke was brilliantly fulfilling the mission of the BBC to *inform, educate and entertain* via his long-running radio series *Letter from America*, I attempted to keep my marriage alive through penning dozens of mostly desperate missives which, although clearly not part of a series, least of all for the purposes of broadcasting, I nevertheless grouped together under the heading of *Letters to Tehran*.

My darling Arash, Azizam,
It's been over two months now and I've had absolutely no news from you. I can't help but wonder what you are doing now that you are back in Banafsheh Street. I do wish that I were with you for I have come to tire of our separation - there is a constant emptiness that seems to have worked its way right inside my bones - I have not got used to being apart. I don't think I ever will. It is hard to imagine what Tehran must be like post-revolution, although we do get glimpses on TV - massive demonstrations and chanting on the streets of Tehran for the most part. From afar it all seems rather frightening. As for me, well, most days my father observes me checking the post, hoping for some sign from you. Even though he has his own views as to what I ought to be doing with my life - fortunately he mostly keeps them to himself - he still seems to share my disappointment when no letter comes my way. It's always the same story when the time comes for the postman to pass. Nothing. Nothing at all. At least not from

you. I know how important it is for you to be out there and far away, hoping to improve the lives of the Iranian people, to make a new and better place for them to live. I can understand all of that. But you should also understand that I miss you, so much. I really need to have news of you. And of the family too. Keep well, be safe. I love you my darling.

Of course it gave my mother no satisfaction to learn that her worries relating to my father's health were well founded or that the preliminary diagnosis issued by the doctors of St. Margaret's hospital in Epping was, as she had suspected from the outset, entirely inaccurate and imprecise. Not that a word of apology was uttered. No, this time the diagnosis had turned full circle. Far from giving my father a clean bill of health, they now had some extremely bad news to deliver, although not within earshot of my father. The same specialist with whom my mother had been obliged to cross swords in order to receive the offer of further tests informed her of the results. His manner was so remote and divorced from any basic notions of compassion or humanity that he could just as easily have been talking about the weather. But he was not. He was talking about my father's life. Or, rather, the ending of his life.

'Yes, I have Mr. Symonds' results with me here now. He has cancer. I would give him about eighteen months max. That should be plenty of time for the two of you to get your affairs in order.'

There was no discussion. No detailed question and answer session. Not the slightest hint of empathy or sorrow.

'You can see my assistant about the range of treatments we propose and what we consider would be the most sensible course of action. It might well be though that he would be better off at the Royal Marsden in south London because that is a specialist cancer hospital. Good day.'

And that was it. My father's death sentence. Eighteen months max, indeed. My parents returned to their home in Loughton, my father in the dark as to the fate which apparently awaited him because, rightly or wrongly, my mother had immediately decided that this would be in

168

his best interests and that in any event he would not want to know. In fact, to begin with she didn't even tell me.

But I too began to think about the notion of the passage of time. How much time would it be right to allocate to making a go of my marriage? Had I not already been generous in its allocation towards Arash? We had first met when I was 19 years old, back in 1972. I had spent four years with him and his family in Iran. The hope then was that a passport would be synonymous with change - but that had not proved to be the case. Nor had Cork or Paris seen my husband being brought back into my embrace. Nor, evidently, had a second marriage done the trick. A good few years had gone by - I was now almost 27 years old and my situation seemed more hopeless than ever. If only there were light at the end of the tunnel. But there was not, only the prospect of more tunnels. For the first time, slowly, I became angry and disturbed. I didn't need my father to tell me - I could see it clearly with my own eyes - that my marriage to Arash was going nowhere fast. If only he could hear me screaming out in frustration then, surely, he would seek to bring about change. Time to put pen to paper again.

Arash,
It's gone midnight. Everyone is in bed. So there is quiet in the house. But there are angry thoughts spinning around in my head and which steadfastly refuse to go away. It was so good when I saw your beautiful script on an envelope containing your long letter. I must have read and re-read that letter at least a hundred times, listening to your words, hearing your voice and laughing at your clever illustrations sketched in between sentences. But those good feelings have now run their course and yet again, I find myself sitting and waiting. Sitting and waiting alone. Is that to be my destiny in life - to sit and wait alone? Just as I did in Iran, in Ireland, in France and now England.

I have finally come to see that it's a pattern belonging not to any one country or a particular situation, but one brought about by you. The morning of our second marriage, you said that you wouldn't change and I chose to ignore your words. That was my mistake. Why do you simply ignore my letters? I just can't understand. I am less able or inclined to hide my frustrations from my parents who remain anxious beyond all measure. But as the weeks and months go by I don't see any end in sight. My mind is in turmoil when I think of my desperate efforts to be with you. Even in Iran it was a permanent battle to be by your side. And since leaving Iran we have been more apart than ever.

I just don't feel any urgency on your part; I get no sense of your desire to be with me. Maybe because there is none. Now, it seems, I am fighting a lonely and losing battle. I always believed that once you were out of Iran, we would finally begin our life as a couple, united and together at all times and, dare I say it, even think of starting a family. God knows I have always desired you, and despite the passage of so many years, I have never stopped being in love with you. Not for one moment.

I understand that your mind is occupied with many things. But I have begged you so often now to send a letter, even a short one, more regularly. One letter every few months is just not good enough. I can't understand how you can simply ignore me. You can't love me. Although I have difficulty in stopping myself, the time for crying is now over. If you don't change in your attitude towards me, I will leave you. I am telling you, Arash, I will leave you. I know that you won't take me seriously, you will probably laugh out loud, why shouldn't you? Because I have always been the one to cling on desperately to our sham of a marriage. But I am serious Arash. Hear me when I tell you that I am serious. I am fed up with you. I am through with acting like a fool. Please hear me, for the sake of our future together. I have always loved you more than I knew I could ever love anyone. But that is wearing thin - you are always so far away. Please write soon.

Another letter from the heart. And, the following morning, another letter torn up, ripped into several pieces, in fact, before being placed in the bin. Leave Arash - the man I love? How on earth had I even been able to contemplate such a proposition? No, the waste-paper basket was where that letter belonged. Thank goodness for the cold light of day.

170

Jeremy Josephs came to see me on 27th July 1980. I remember the date because it was the day the Shah of Iran died from complications relating to non-Hodgkin lymphoma, the blood cancer from which he had been suffering for some time. He had been granted permanent asylum in Egypt by the country's President, Anwar El Sadat. The Shah was just sixty years old - five years younger than my father. President Sadat saw to it that the Shah was given a state funeral - one of the reasons, perhaps, why he would himself be assassinated by Muslim extremists barely fifteen months after the Shah's demise. Jeremy had by now been called to the Bar - but only with a view to acquiring a professional qualification. His real interest, like Arash's, lay in politics and he was very upbeat that day because he was poised to take up a position as political assistant to the leader of the Liberal Party, the Rt. Hon David Steel MP. He said that such a description made his future sound far grander than it was likely to be - bag carrier and general dog's body might be more accurate, he joked. It did not take him long to pick up on his familiar refrain. Where is your husband? What about your dancing? And it did not take me long to roll out my familiar answers - that things were uncertain, the situation unclear.

'Listen', he said, 'I don't know anything about ballet. But I am very keen to find out. What I suggest we do is take the tube up to London together and you start attending professional classes again. I just feel that you are wasting your time teaching keep-fit in Essex. You've told me of your passion for dancing. I'd really love to see you dance. I've never been to a ballet class before. Besides, I want to see you back where you belong - on the stage.'

That's how I managed to get myself back into the world of ballet. By regularly going to classes at the Urdang Academy of Dance in London's Covent Garden and where I came under the watchful eye of an inspirational Russian teacher I knew only as Yelena. How wonderful it was to take out my ballet shoes again, to warm up at the *barre*, be put through my balletic paces before completing the class to a series of *grandes jetées* as Yelena's pianist, retained for the ninety minutes, thumped out classical music at the Urdang Academy's rather run down premises in Shelton Street. It was as if I had come home.

I became accustomed to spending sleepless nights contemplating my situation in the lounge of my parents' home. I preferred that to tossing and turning in bed. Their lounge became a kind of ad hoc nocturnal study where I would write out long and rambling letters to Arash - at least half of which would fail to find their way into the postal system. One night my father surprised me by coming to join me. He might not have been aware of the precise details of his illness - certainly the word cancer was never spoken out loud - but he was nevertheless perfectly well aware that he had a battle of his own on his hands. Sleep eluded him too. 'Clair darling, I thought I could hear you in the sitting room. What are you doing up at this hour?' He sat down in an armchair close to me. 'I guess you can't sleep either - is there anything in particular on your mind?' I had always been reluctant to open up and expose my vulnerability to my father. Especially because his reservations about the suitability of Arash as a husband seemed to have been proved spot on. But never once had he sought to point a recriminatory finger at me, never once did he utter those awful words *I told you so*. And still he could not bear to see his daughter aching with sorrow. In the eerie quiet of the early morning hours, it seemed easier to lower barriers and as we sat next to one another the words flowed with ease. 'I miss Arash, daddy, but at the same time I'm angry with him too. I'm confused, I don't know what to do. It makes my moods go up and down like a yo-yo - I am sure you must have noticed - so I'm sorry if it's not always been easy having me around.'

'Don't be so silly, Clair, my darling. I am sure this medication I am on has made me have my ups and downs too. Listen, why don't you ring Arash in the morning? Have a chat together - speak to him and perhaps that will help you see things more clearly.'

I heard my father. But the truth was I wanted more than a phone call. I wanted more than an airmail letter. I wanted my husband.

'Daddy, I know you aren't going to like this. But I am just wondering if it wouldn't be best for me to fly out to Tehran and be with him.' I heard his silence all too clearly. Then I heard him breathe a heavy sigh. He had seen me make more than my fair share of decisions which ran contrary to his better judgement. Despite that he had always gone out of his way to confer upon me the freedom to pursue a pathway of my own choosing. But now he could no longer hold his tongue. He too spoke freely and without restraint. 'Clair, my darling, you and I both know that at the moment Iran is a country in great turmoil - an Islamic Republic being run by the Mullahs and the Ayatollah Khomeini. That doesn't bode well for you as a young foreign Jewish girl. My paramount concern is for your safety. So I would have to advise you strongly against going back to Iran just now. It simply won't be safe.' We sat together in silence for a while. Then my father continued. He needed to unburden himself more. He put his hand on mine and continued quietly.

'Clair, I am begging you to listen to me. I am pleading with you from my heart. I am looking at you now and beginning to feel that at long last you are starting to raise your head above the water - even though it's clearly difficult for you being estranged from Arash. My very strong feeling is that if you do insist on going back to Tehran then not only will you be in great danger but that you will sink right down to the bottom. Except this time you will not come back up again.'

Chapter 25: In a Bubble of Happiness

There are few things more brutal in life, at least in terms of the speed at which a dancer's hopes and aspirations may be dashed, than an audition. An audition, I soon came to learn, also happens to be a setting where words have a habit of being deceptive. For whereas in normal circumstances you would assume that the phrase *thank you* is harmless enough and intended primarily to convey a message of gratitude or appreciation, at an audition precisely the opposite is the case - it is dance talk for being informed that your prospects are over and would you please leave the studio forthwith. But no thank you seemed to be coming my way in the autumn of 1980 at the Pineapple Dance Studios in Covent Garden, one of the UK's premier dance centres for castings and rehearsals. Whilst others were being given their marching orders in rapid succession - *thank you, thank you, thank you* - I was apparently surviving the cull.

No special briefing was required to put you on your guard - you could see from his no-nonsense demeanour that Udo Badstübner was not a man to be messed with. He was an established German-British dancer and choreographer who had plucked the stage name Alexander Roy out of thin air. Together with his Australian-born wife Christina Gallea, a distinguished dancer in her own right, they had established the Alexander Roy London Ballet Theatre, an itinerant company which toured extensively around the world performing at the most exotic spots imaginable. It also happened to be based in North House, Eton Avenue - a most magnificent red-brick mansion in London's stylish Swiss Cottage - a perfect job opportunity for me and the main reason, therefore, that I was anxious not to be thanked.

All that remained for me was to get through an informal interview at the end of the audition.

'Thank you very much Clair', Alexander said, his middle-European accent not difficult to detect. 'That was very nice - I can see that you have had some Russian training. You know we are a hard-working company - we don't have a permanent base which means that we are away more often than not. Sometimes in the UK but very often overseas. Would that be a problem for you?'

'No, no, not at all', I replied. 'I think it would do me good to get away from time to time.'

'I see you have experience in both Ireland and Iran. Tell me - how old are you?'

'I'm 23', I replied, hoping that he would not detect the sudden rush of blood to my cheeks for having given myself a perhaps overly-generous reduction of four years.

When I returned home to tell my parents that I had a new job, they were thrilled for me. They both said the same thing - that it would herald a new beginning.

That was the good news. The bad news was that my father's physical condition had taken a significant turn for the worse. For most of his life he had been fortunate to have enjoyed good health and had little inclination or desire to dwell on sickness, be it others' or his own. He had developed his own inimitable style in this regard; *I trust you are well* becoming his catchphrase, its great beauty, he thought, that it pre-empted the possibility of having to listen to a potentially protracted list of other people's ailments. But he could now no longer ignore the state of his own rapidly deteriorating health. The dozen or so pills laid out before him every morning were a stark reminder of what kept him alive, although use of the word cancer - *the C word* was the closest one could come - remained strictly taboo in my parents' home. Stiff upper lip and putting on a brave face at all times, he steadfastly refused to give in to the loss of appetite, tiredness, and innumerable other debilitating side effects of the drug Interferon, administered to encourage communication between cells and with a view to triggering the protective defences of his immune system. His obstinate determination remained a constant as he went about his business calls, taking next to no time off from his job as an expert insurance assessor with the Sun Alliance group. In his spare time he would put his considerable engineering skills to good use at home, producing on his lathe every single working part of a brass clock known as a Congreve, its distinguishing feature that it uses a ball rolling along a zigzag track rather than a pendulum to regulate the time and the creation of which he had every intention of completing.

To those who refuse to accept that the life of a professional ballet dancer is not the most romantic career imaginable then a glimpse of a day in the life of the ARLBT – no one ever had the energy to say the words Alexander Roy London Ballet Theatre out loud - should help to disabuse that notion. Endless drives around Britain's overcrowded motorway network, overnight stops at run down B & Bs and a series of venues which hardly entitled you to announce to the world that you had hit the big time - the Courtyard in Hereford, the Arts Theatre in Cambridge, the Playhouse in Derby, the Theatre Royal in Lincoln - to name but a few. ARLBT was almost unique in that it operated within the world of unsubsidised theatre, which had the benefit of conferring upon its directors artistic independence and autonomy. But the downside was that Alex and Christina were obliged to run the company on a shoestring. Unable to finance the hiring of any administrative or technical personnel, they ended up doing almost everything themselves. We would regularly set off mid-morning, arrive at a venue a few hours before the performance was due to get underway, settle into the dressing rooms, carry out a warm up class, run through last-minute rehearsals, complete the performance, take a bow, down a quick drink at the bar before clambering back into the white Fiat minibus waiting outside. Only then to begin the long and arduous journey back to Swiss Cottage, with Alexander Roy, our director, choreographer, ballet-master, task-master, pay-master - and now *chauffeur* - at the wheel. We would often arrive back in London in the middle of the night, exhausted. No, the everyday life of an ARLBT dancer was not romantic at all. Still, it was wonderful to be working as a professional dancer again. Being part of a small touring company - there were only ever around ten of us at any one time - also enabled me to perform a wide variety of new roles - Titania, Queen of the Fairies in *A Midsummer Night's Dream* and the life-size dancing doll in the sentimental comic ballet *Coppélia*. Alex's apparently limitless energy as reflected in the company's frenetic programme was precisely what was required in terms of taking my mind off of my marital woes.

I went to visit my father at the Royal Marsden, the first hospital in the world to have devoted its entire resources to the fight against cancer. I walked into a bright and airy ward containing six beds, only half of which were occupied. I glanced towards the one nearest the window where my father was lying, his eyes focused on nothing in particular, his thoughts well beyond the boundaries of the hospital walls. Despite my short absence, I was shocked at his weight loss, his ashen face, his cheeks that had become drawn and sallow. When he caught sight of me I immediately saw that familiar dogged determination hidden behind his effortless smile and I kissed him gently on his cheek. 'How are you, Clair? I have missed you. Tell me, did your tour up north go well darling? Mum and I want to come to watch you dance - perhaps when you are a little closer to London.' 'Daddy', I said, hoping that he wouldn't have noticed the uncharacteristic low croak in my voice and pulling up a chair to be close to him. I cleared my throat and began again. 'Daddy, that would be good, I want to see you out of here - the sooner the better.'

He put his hand on mine and smiled. 'Oh', he said after a brief pause, and with an unexpected lightness in his voice. 'Look here darling, look at this.' And he reached over for the Sunday Times on his bedside table. I wondered what might have retained his interest in the news this week - something relating to Iran, perhaps. Then, raising the paper up with his two hands, as if holding a prayer book, his olive green eyes looked directly into my face. 'You will never believe who brought me this a couple of days ago.' Whereupon he said nothing more, as he searched into my face, challenging me to come up with a convincing reply. 'Nope, daddy, I'm sorry, you've got me.' 'Jeremy Josephs', he said, obviously delighted that the correct answer had eluded me. I was astonished at his reply. 'Yes, Jeremy', he repeated, 'he paid me a surprise visit and brought this newspaper to help occupy my time. We even did some of the crossword together. He stayed a while', my father continued, 'but he had to go off after an hour or so. Likes the law, apparently, but none too keen on the wig', he joked. And in a barely audible voice he reflected, 'nice lad that Jeremy'. After a short interlude he continued - but in a less reflective tone, 'anyway, darling, tell me, any news of Arash recently?'

I knew my father asked after his son-in-law with a heavy heart and now, for once, I took it upon myself to lift his spirits. I pulled the chair closer to the bed so that we could speak with more privacy. 'Daddy,' I said, taking hold of his thin hand, 'I am thinking of leaving Arash'. He looked at me barely able to take in what I had just said. So I said it again. 'I'm thinking of leaving Arash. Now that I have found a job for myself and after so many years of either stop-start or being apart, I can see that I am able to stand on my own two feet, that I can manage alone and, well, I like it.' My father eased himself up in the bed. It was as if a heavy load had been lifted from his shoulders. 'Clair, my darling, you have just made me a very happy man. We must do whatever it takes to get a divorce. Pass me a pen and paper and we'll write out a list of what needs to be done. Now, listen to me, I don't want you to start worrying about anything to do with costs - I will pay for the best solicitor. Just get the ball rolling - and do it right away.' As he put his arms around me I could feel how thin he had become. 'Clair, I hope I am not sounding too upbeat about this, because I am sure that this must have been a difficult decision for you. But this is the greatest gift you could ever have given to me. My darling, of course you can't see it but I can tell you right now that I am in one huge bubble of happiness.'

As I left the Royal Marsden and set off down the Fulham Road on the journey back to Loughton, I was happy that my news had boosted my father's morale. But I also felt a fraud. I had never mentioned the word divorce - he had. I had never thought of retaining the services of a solicitor - he had. The truth was that I had only spoken of separation because I thought it was what he wanted to hear. Yet with his health so evidently broken, I could not bear to contemplate the possibility of his leaving this world with his heart broken too. I resolved to look through the Yellow Pages in search of a solicitor - like that on my next visit to the Royal Marsden I would have something positive to report, at least from my father's perspective.

Sunderland, Hartlepool, Middlesbrough and Darlington might not have been Britain's most glamorous venues - but who cared when you knew that the ARLBT would be giving seasons not just in several countries on continental Europe but Malta, Brunei, Sarawak, India and Taiwan? It was a programme of overseas travel with which the larger companies simply could not compete. We were nimble, footloose and fancy-free. You soon forgot about the Arena Theatre in Wolverhampton, which often struggled to fill its 150 seats, when you were booked to perform at the Chiang Kai Shek Cultural Center in Taipei with its capacity of over 2000. I admired Alex and Christina not just for their drive and energy but for being able to pull off such a feat. We became accustomed to handing over our passports to Christina who oversaw visa applications and travel arrangements. I remember my embarrassment when Alex handed mine back to me in the spring of 1981, as we were preparing to leave for our south-east Asia tour. With a twinkle in his eye and indicating that no reply would be required on my part, he simply said '23 years old indeed!'

My father passed away on 19th August of that year. In fact the doctor at St. Margaret's hospital in Epping had got it right - he had fought and battled against his unmentionable illness for eighteen months, precisely as predicted. He was cremated two days later at Golders Green crematorium in Hoop Lane. Needless to say Arash was not by my side to support me in my process of mourning. Why should he have been? What was new? What had changed? Nothing. But a letter of condolence arrived in due course. Letters from his parents and sisters also found their way to Loughton. I placed them all alongside my large bundle of missives to and from Tehran.

Back home in Loughton the silver-coloured ball of my father's Congreve clock ran down the zigzag track he had meticulously cut out on his lathe. It would take about 20 seconds, on average, to complete its run before tripping an escapement mechanism which would in turn reverse the tilt of the tray and cause the hands of the clock to move forward. As that ball journeyed back and forth I could hear him speaking to me, his message louder and clearer than ever before.

Chapter 26: Covent Garden tube
London, May 1982

In the spring of 1982 I returned from a ten day stint at the Valletta Royal Opera House, situated in the heart of the Maltese capital and where the ARLBT had been performing an innovative ballet choreographed by Alex to the hauntingly beautiful music of Albinoni's Adagio in G minor. Usually my mother's first question would have been to enquire how the tour had gone. But that day she did not. She simply said that she had big news.

'Arash is out of Iran'.

'Arash is out of Iran', I repeated, astonished.

'That's right, he's out of Iran'.

'So where is he then?'

'He's in London'.

'In London, oh my God.'

I knew that we had to meet up right away. I thought that in view of our prolonged separation, a meeting on neutral territory would be most appropriate. Since Covent Garden had come to be synonymous with the London world of dance, I decided upon that area.

Prior to setting off for our rendezvous I sat down to have a word with my mother. Since leaving South Africa she had continued her work as a choreographer and her greatest success, the one which would come to define her career, was to have been responsible for staging the entire production of the hit musical *Ipi Tombi* and with which she enjoyed worldwide success, notably in the West End of London and on Broadway in New York. Set in the apartheid era, the musical told the story of a young black man leaving his village and wife to work in the mines of Johannesburg. *Ipi Tombi* was a corruption of the Zulu words *iphi intombi* which translate into English as '*where is the girl?*' They were words which happened to be relevant to me that day.

'Mum, if you don't hear from me again it's not because I haven't wanted to come back or that I have gone away. It's because something has happened to me.'

My mother could hardly believe her ears. 'Clair, what on earth are you talking about?' I explained that at the back of my mind I had a worry, that some of Arash's letters had been so rambling and incoherent, so chaotic in content and far removed from the reality of what had happened to us as a couple, that I had on occasions come to question the state of his mental health. 'So if I don't come back you should do all that is necessary to find out what has happened to me. I am sure everything will be fine though. I am sorry to pass that anxiety on to you, but I didn't want to leave until I had got it off of my chest.' It had been over two years since Arash left me with my parents in Loughton to find his way in the new Iran. During that period feelings of optimism and expectation, anger and frustration, love and despair had all criss-crossed my mind. Now, as I entered the lift taking me to the arranged meeting place at Covent Garden tube, on the corner of Long Acre and James Street, I felt more than a little apprehensive. I took a few deep breaths in an attempt to centre myself for this rendezvous, so long overdue. It was there that I saw a man standing with his back to me. I immediately recognised the silhouette of my husband. As he walked towards me I saw, for the first time, perhaps, that his comportment seemed less certain, his stature somehow diminished. He appeared not to stand as proud or tall as the man I remembered from Talar Roudaki. Or was it rather that I had changed? All of these feelings within just a few seconds. Yet as we kissed hello I knew immediately that I was back with the man I had loved for so long.

It seemed ridiculous to feel awkward in each other's company. But we did. To begin with we wandered aimlessly around the area which had come to be dominated by trendy shops and street performers but most spectacularly of all, the grand cobbled piazza of Covent Garden market. After a while we agreed that it was not a walk around London's major tourist sites that was required but a talk. Fortunately there was an abundance of coffee shops and we settled down in one adjacent to the Royal Opera House and from where it was possible to could catch a glimpse of Enzo Plazzotta's bronze statue *Young Dancer*, her head down in reflective mode as if she too were contemplating her future. It was as well that this particular establishment offered free top-ups of hot drinks because it seemed clear that we were set for a long afternoon.

It didn't take Arash long to admit that he was disappointed with the politics of the Islamic Republic, where anyone who might happen to oppose the new regime was given short shrift. In that respect the land ruled by the Ayatollah Khomeini had come to share much common ground with that of the old Iran presided over by the Shah. The Revolution was not what he had hoped it would be. I considered that my tales of balletic travel with the Alexander Roy London Ballet Theatre were positively dull compared to the political upheaval that had taken place in Iran. But I rattled through them nevertheless - I spoke mostly about our performances at the Tata Theatre in Bombay, on the not unreasonable grounds that it was likely to sound more enticing and exotic than an overnight stop at a bottom of the range guest house in Sunderland followed by a five hour trip back down the A1 and which was, rather appropriately, the longest running road in the UK. It was all too obvious though that we were both steadfastly refusing to address the central issue. What had become of our marriage? What of us? It was time, finally, to talk from the heart. To my surprise, Arash indicated that he would like to be the one to begin, although his first remarks rather caught me off-guard.

'I am sorry if, in the past, I made some disparaging remarks about the Holocaust. That was wrong of me. I wouldn't wish you to think of me as some sort of crazed revisionist. It's something I have thought about a lot and I hope you can forgive me.'

'Of course I can forgive you, Arash. But what you may have said about the plight of European Jewry has not been at the forefront of my mind. It's not that I would wish in any way to seek to diminish the enormity of the plight of the six million - rather that today I am really more interested in talking about the two of us. Because I have missed you. You can't imagine how much. Or maybe you can.'

'I have missed you too Clair *jaan*. I know that I have made mistakes - perhaps we both have - and I am sorry for that too. I want you to believe me when I say that I am going to change. I really am. It's my intention now to finally finish my architectural studies. What I hope to do then is to build flats for each member of the family on the land next to our house in Banafsheh Street and sign the drawings off in my own name.'

As I held a second hot mug of freshly ground coffee between my hands, it was all too easy to picture myself once again in the warm embrace of the Alizadeh family. I remembered their generosity of spirit and thought of the constant stream of warmth and affection they had shown me during my years in Tehran. As I travelled down memory lane one hour quickly became two, two became three and the conversation, stilted and awkward at first, now flowed free and fast. It was as if we had never been apart. As our exchanges found a natural rhythm of their own, so the spark between us was reignited and I found myself drawn like a magnet into the gaze of Arash's sensitive eyes, attracted to his strong fine-looking face and adoring the natural charm of his slightly accented English. I knew at that moment why I had always loved him. I couldn't help myself. I had been a hopeless addict, the chemistry of our relationship my drug, my troublesome fix sitting right there at the table before me.

Of course I didn't know it at the time, but as the early evening approached and I had still not returned to Loughton, my mother was becoming increasingly concerned for my safety. Where was I? Why had I not called to let her know that I would be late? She decided that if I had not returned by 9 pm she would ring the police, although unsure as to precisely what she might be reporting. Meanwhile, in a Covent Garden coffee shop her son-in-law remained in full flow.

'Clair, I've already fixed up a separate living space in Banafsheh Street, away from the rest of the family. I've put up curtains and arranged the room - my mother helped me. I know that she would love to see you again - we have all missed you so much. Clair, come back to Tehran with me. We can begin again. What do you say, Clair *jaan*?'

Slowly but surely I was being courted and seduced again. I was uncertain if I would be able to resist because Arash was overwhelming me with a package of all I had ever wanted to hear - an acknowledgement of his mistakes, independent living accommodation, a renewed commitment to our marriage, a fresh start. Was there anything else he could possibly come up with to encourage me to sign on the dotted line?

As a matter of fact there was - as my erstwhile Iranian knight knew very well. He readied himself, aware that he was poised to play his trump card.

'And there's one more thing Clair. You are 29, I am well into my thirties - and I do think that the time is now right...'

'Right for what?' I interrupted. I knew very well what he was going to say. But I wanted him to spell it out clearly. I had been waiting the best part of ten years to hear this.

'It's just that I do think that the time is now right for us to start a family. Wouldn't it be a wonderful new beginning for us both if, in a year or so, we were blessed with a baby?'

And then I heard it. It was the rolling sound of a metal ball. A stainless steel metal ball, relentlessly making its way back and forth along the zigzag tracking of my father's magnificent brass Congreve clock. It was as if he were there right next to me in the coffee shop, the three of us sitting together. I heard him speaking to me, his message equally loud and clear. His words were not difficult to recall - they were etched permanently into my subconscious mind - *Clair, darling, if you go back to Tehran you will sink right down to the bottom except this time you won't come back up again.* I had spent over a decade steadfastly ignoring his heartfelt pleas, doing my own thing, going my own way. Would I continue in such a fashion?

Arash had been at his most convincing, aware that this was his last roll of the dice. At times I was tempted to seize what he was now offering - to snatch it firmly with both hands whilst still within my grasp.

Whatever the case, it was time now, finally, to make up my mind. In the event I found that the words came rather easily.

'Arash, everything you have said is what I always wanted to hear. I was desperate to hear you speak in this way. You made me experience feelings and sensations of such intensity for so many years. People found it difficult to understand my love. That didn't bother me - I always held on, never wanting to let you go, because I was so in love with you. I even talked you into a second marriage thinking that would ensure you remained by my side. But I have had to learn to let you go. Believe me when I tell you that this is not something that comes easily to me. And yet it's something I have to do. Not because it's what my father always wished for. But for me. For my own sanity. All of what you have said, well, it's just come too late. I waited for so many years for things to come right. I waited for you in Tehran, Cork, Paris and now these two last years in London. I can't run the risk of waiting another ten. I just can't. I'm sorry Arash, but it's over.'

We walked back towards Covent Garden tube and the Piccadilly line, from where we would be going our separate ways. I would be heading north towards Holborn and then Loughton-bound on the central line, Arash in a southerly direction and back to the West End. And from there on I knew not where. What I did know was that we would be unlikely to see one another again. One would have thought from the awkward silence between us that there was nothing more to say. But the truth was that our minds were both full of the most powerful emotions and silent dialogues of their own. Of course I don't know what expression I wore on my face - I could only observe Arash's countenance and saw a proud man full of regrets, reeling with remorse, pain and sorrow. We took one of the four lifts down towards the platforms. It was there Arash started to speak, taking my hand as he did so.

'I am really sorry for what I have done Clair. You will never know quite how much. I know that I didn't always treat you properly. You deserved better than that.' He paused, his eyes heavy. 'Look after yourself, *khoda-hafez* - goodbye.'

186

I was so choked up with emotion I struggled to respond.

'Arash, there was no one ever better than you. It wasn't just your fault. Nothing is ever one way. I had my part to play in all of this; I have been responsible for my own actions, although they were only ever based on my love for you. It doesn't really matter whose fault it was anyway. I am very sorry as well. Look after yourself too.'

A sudden rush of incoming air and rattling of the metal tracks indicated that my train would be the first to arrive. Whatever was going to take place between us now had to happen quickly. Not that it was anything extraordinary. We kissed - not as lovers but on the cheek as friends do. We hugged one another goodbye, our gaze refusing to part even as the doors slammed together tight.

As my train headed towards the darkness of the tunnel deep below the streets of London, I could see Arash standing there, his face taut and blank, that image becoming blurred and soon disappearing as the tube gathered pace and momentum. The tunnel announced its arrival by a dramatic change in sound and light. Finally the tables had turned. It was the first time I had walked away.